THE CRADLE

OF THE

RAPTOR

BOOK ONE:

The Beginning

T.L. HERSHEY

NEWMAN SPRINGS PUBLISHING
320 Broad Street
Red Bank, NJ 07701

First originally published by Newman Springs Publishing 2018

ISBN 978-1-64096-394-8 (Paperback)
ISBN 978-1-64096-395-5 (Digital)

Printed in the United States of America

DEDICATION

To those who have also lived this story, this is for you.

CONTENTS

FOREWORD

This story has been hard to chronicle and will, for many of you, be equally difficult to read. We would much rather travel through the Norman-Rockwell-type stories than walk the dark paths with those who have suffered. But we will never conquer an enemy unless we find the strength to look deep into its eyes.

Life as we live it is all about perspective. Our perspective becomes the reality in which we live. This story is told from the perspective of a frightened little boy as he lived it from the cradle to age thirteen. It is told as accurately as possible without attempting to exaggerate or embellish. Much of the dialogue is near-verbatim; the rest has been necessarily reconstructed. Names of people and places have been changed to protect privacy. Others from that saga will have differing perspectives, but this is the story I lived. It was a good launching pad for the highly adventurous and often incredibly painful life I have lived, and through good times and bad, it was all worthwhile!

—*Michael Raptor*

PROLOGUE

He stood motionless in the shadows of the majestic oak trees shading the edge of the small town park from the early morning heat.

A smile slowly formed on his tanned face as he watched a pair of early-rising boys shooting baskets and scrambling for rebounds despite the already near-eighty-degree temperature. The world, he thought, will always belong to the young, and the naive! It was as it should be. The smile spread to his dark eyes as he remembered.

The strongest impressions were the horses and the ever-present fear—not fear of the horses—for he held an inherited lifetime passion for horses. It was something vaguer, an indefinable shadow in some corner of his subconsciousness, always lurking, always there, ready to paralyze his small body and mind. It was gone now, but it had once ruined his life!

The story of the earliest origins of the fear had been buried for years. He may never have learned of it if he hadn't picked up a small religious publication by a well-known international evangelist. *Was it fate, destiny, or just the way life works?* he wondered.

The pamphlet had been small and unobtrusive; he had picked it up at a missionary guesthouse on a sweltering afternoon in Cape Coast, Africa. As his eyes skimmed the opening lines, he froze. The words, Timber Lake, South Dakota, leaped out at him and with it a tidal wave of memories and more than a few unanswered questions, ghosts from his past! He read and reread the article, knowing instinctively that this was the beginning of the path to the answers he sought. Thoughtfully, he picked up a pen and legal pad and began to write, "Dear Grandma."

The answers had come slowly and painfully at times, but gradually over the next eight years, the story emerged from the shadows of the murky past. The fear had been born in the womb!

THE GIFT

Charlotte stood at the chipped porcelain sink of her kitchen in the small, gray stucco house nestled in the South Dakota pines. Her life had been hard, and she had no real prospects for improvement any time soon. She sighed and rested her swollen stomach against the sink as she surveyed the frigid, white landscape beyond her kitchen window. It was, she thought, as cold and bare as her soul!

Her mind scrolled back to the scenes of the previous evening, and she felt goose bumps form. The pastor's house had been filled to overflowing, and the noise of worshippers had steadily increased to a low roar, punctuated by occasional screams as another worshipper got "the gift." She had finally convinced Carl to bring her home, but he had immediately returned to the gathering, leaving her alone in the cold darkness.

A slow shudder ran through her thin body as she relived the past few weeks. Their calm little chapel had been seized in the grip of radical "revivalism," and suddenly, her whole world was twisting and shaking. Besides the unpredictable and boisterous behavior, there were unexplainable supernatural happenings, including prophesies coming true before their very eyes. The movement had begun among the young people who had ended up congregating in the pastor's house where the visitations and manifestations had continued non-stop for more than a week.

Charlotte and her handsome husband, Carl Raptor, had been swept along with the spiritual euphoria and had shouted and danced with the rest of the young worshippers. But where she had become increasingly doubtful and eventually fearful of the movement, Carl continued to be totally consumed by his role as one of the prophets;

and despite their love and deep commitment to each other, at times, she felt she barely knew him anymore. Sometimes, she even feared him!

Her thin body relaxed, and a shadow of a smile touched her face as she remembered her and Carl. What a romance! He was a muscular man, medium height, with a stocky frame and a too-handsome face. She had loved his practical jokes and fine sense of humor, but had realized early in their relationship that he was no match for her inherited intellect and emotional strength. The one thing that had bothered her was his uncontrollable anger. He could explode with the fury of a lava-spewing volcano as quickly as he could gather her into his powerful arms for a tender kiss. He was a contradiction in human emotions.

She really couldn't blame him, she thought. He had had a hard childhood as an illegitimate child in a day when the shame of illegitimacy was nearly unbearable. But that was all behind him now, as a father of two with another on the way.

She gave a sudden surprised gasp as the baby inside her gave a vigorous kick. Another boy, she was sure. This one was different somehow though, she reflected. There were long periods where he would be so still she feared for his health. That would always be during the times when she was in the grip of the paralyzing fear. Was he instinctively trying to make it easy for her at these times? She wondered. Or was he also suffering from her terror? A short wave of resentment washed over her. Why did she have to be pregnant again with two small boys and all the terrifying events of the church making her life an almost daily horror? How would it all end? Would it just go on forever? Was this to be her life?

She turned from the sink and reached for the shiny, galvanized water bucket. The well with its ancient hand pump was just outside the door, but in this frigid northland, it was necessary to bundle up even if going for a bucket of water. She hoped Carl would be home in time for breakfast. *Our boys*, she thought, *needed a father more than the church needed a prophet.*

They were nearly finished with breakfast when she heard the crunch of the battered Chevy's tires on the snow in the lane. The porch door slammed, and the kitchen door opened to admit a tired-looking Carl. Weary though he was, a gleam still shone in his intense gray eyes. He had not wanted to leave the pastor's house, but the cows needed milking. Without a word, he pulled out his chair at the head of the table, sat and bowed his head to offer a silent prayer, and then began to eat.

The boys had finished their breakfast and sat silently observing him. Carl Jr., the oldest and the most frequent object of his angry outbursts, slowly squirmed from his chair and escaped to the living room, followed at length by his brother Randy. They knew enough to avoid any unnecessary contact with their father when he was tired or stressed.

Quietly, they stood on the large floor register soaking up the warmth from the huge wood furnace in the basement. Soon, the murmur of their parents' voices in the next room began to rise in pitch and stridency.

"Carl, we must stop going to these meetings!" Charlotte said, her voice somewhere between pleading and desperate. "We never know what's going to happen."

"Can't you see?!" Carl nearly shouted. "That's how it is when the Spirit is in control!"

Choking on her sobs, Charlotte rose and began to gather the dirty breakfast dishes from the table.

"Come on, boys," Carl said, rising from his chair at the head of the table. "There's work to do before school."

Mennonite Revival

It was Wednesday evening again, the night for the weekly gathering at the little Timber Lake Chapel. Sensing their father's tension, the family was silent during the fifteen-minute drive over the rough dirt road. Something big was going down—they knew—but what?

Carl Jr. was enjoying the little thrills of anticipation as he stared out the grimy backseat window. He was always ready for another adventure, and tonight, he figured the prospects were good! He grinned unconsciously as he remembered the action at the pastor's house a few evenings earlier when the preacher was so excited he began shouting and jumping up and down in the living room with his clenched fist fully extended in the air. He never even knew he was punching holes in the ceiling tiles as Carl Jr. gleefully took a silent tally—six casualties at final count. Oh yeah! That had been an evening well spent. He later overheard the adults remarking how, when the new replacement tiles were installed, they formed a perfect cross.

Randy, however, with his gentler nature was completely tuned to his mother's silent fear. Although he didn't fully understand her fear, there was a special though unspoken bond between them, and he absorbed her emotions as his own. This evening promised no enjoyment for him.

He felt the old Chevy slow, and suddenly, a clearing appeared in the unbroken wall of towering pine trees on the right side of the gravel road, revealing a small, plain gray stucco chapel. Carl parked beside the rest of the worn and battered cars, and together, they climbed the unpainted concrete front steps and entered the sanctuary. Their feet made clopping sounds on the varnished hardwood floor as they made their way up the aisle to their customary plain handmade pew.

The service began as they all had in the last few weeks. Charlotte felt the familiar knot of fear grow in the pit of her stomach as the crescendo grew. Suddenly, the heavy oak door at the rear of the chapel burst open, and three somber Mennonite bishops strode to the front of the chapel. The head bishop's expression was austere as he mounted the podium, taking the proceedings out of the charge of Pastor Wally. Deathly silence reigned for a few minutes as he surveyed the assembly. Charlotte couldn't breathe; she sat transfixed by the unfolding drama.

Slowly in sonorous tones, the head bishop began to speak. "We have been informed"—he began—"of unacceptable worship practices occurring in this congregation. We are here to investigate these reports. Our Mennonite faith does not approve of miracles and dabbling into the supernatural, and it is our purpose to bring this congregation back into proper practices."

A small ray of hope appeared on Charlotte's horizon. Could it be that after all these weeks of terror, life might return to normal again? "Oh please, God," she breathed. "Let it happen!" She looked again at the austere man in the dark suit standing stiffly on the podium. He looked like an avenging angel; could this be her deliverance? Then, her glance shifted to Pastor Wally. He was a young man who had always been dearly loved by this congregation where he had been ordained to serve. He was, she knew, completely dedicated to his ministry and to these people. He was also totally convinced that God was leading this small band of believers into an era of miracles and manifestations like those the early church. What if he was right? Was life "in the Spirit" supposed to be this scary?

Her mind refocused on the bishop on the podium. She had always viewed him as rather pompous, full of his own importance. Now, however, she felt relief and a sense of hope beginning to trickle into her soul like the first trickles of water from the ancient hand pump outside her house. Maybe life could return to normal!

Suddenly, an authoritative voice boomed from her side, making her jump. "Everyone to your knees to pray!" Carl shouted. Charlotte was aghast. Carl in public was shy and reserved, but this Carl was the one that lately she knew less and less.

The head bishop stood helplessly as the congregation scrambled to their knees. As the noise of the ascending prayers grew louder, he gathered his two colleagues, and they silently exited the building to discuss the situation.

After a lengthy period of boisterous prayer, Carl's voice boomed out again. "Everyone stand and praise the Lord with all your might!"

Charlotte's heart felt like it was made of lead as the people rose from their knees and began to shout and dance. There was no hope!

Sometime later, the door opened to admit the head bishop. He strode to the podium and raised his hand for silence. As the noise dwindled, he began to speak.

"We have conferred," he stated. "And these practices *shall not* continue here!"

He turned on his heel and made an attempt at a dignified exit. Charlotte heard the start of their car's engine, and her brief ray of hope faded with the receding sound of their car as it was gradually swallowed by the gloomy shadows of the pine trees along the rough dirt road. Now, there were only the renewed shouts and writhing of the worshippers around her. She wondered with despair which would crack first, her heart or her mind?

The next week went by in a blur of work squeezed into the cracks between the round-the-clock events unfolding in Pastor Wally's house. To his credit, she had to admit that the young and intense pastor had never pressured anyone to participate in the events at his house. In fact, they had been initiated by young people from the church, and he had at first been reluctant to sanction them. But when he received "the gift" and special revelation, he felt he could only lead out in the unpredictable course of events. And so the shouting, prophesies, and supernatural revelations continued. Charlotte thought with growing despair, *Her two small sons would live in confusion and uncertainty*, while the little one in her, *Was he okay?* she wondered with a sudden pang of fear. He was kicking her less and less as the date neared for his entry into this tumultuous world. Her hands automatically went to her swollen middle, and she pressed firmly. *Was that a movement?* She waited breathlessly until it came again— harder this time. A slight reassuring bump, a gentle reassurance to her that all would be well. She sighed with relief. In a few weeks, he would arrive, a tiny helpless bundle to be held, fed, and cared for. There would be some normality in her world!

It was past noon when she heard the heavy tread of Carl's boots in the porch. He had been gone for a couple hours this morning with no explanation of his activities. As he came through the door, she glanced at his drawn face. He badly needed more real rest, she knew. "There is a special meeting at the church tonight," he said without preamble. "Things are coming to a head."

Coming to a head, she mused almost bitterly. *I wonder what that means.*

The atmosphere was incredibly tense as they entered the little chapel. The front pew where Pastor Wally's family always sat was occupied by the three ministers who had visited earlier. Pastor Wally and his family were not present.

The service began with an unenthusiastic hymn, after which the head bishop stood to address the little group.

"As you know"—he began in his cadaverous voice—"we as a conference cannot tolerate the events of the past few weeks. We have excommunicated Pastor Wally for his refusal to renounce these events and will be providing you with an interim pastor. We realize that many of you are deeply involved as well, and we will require each of you individually to publicly renounce these events as the work of Satan among you."

Charlotte felt Carl stiffen at her side and felt a stab of fear. *Would he do this, or would he choose rather to be an outcast with Pastor Wally and his loyal supporters?* He had always been a deeply spiritual man. He now faced the ultimate spiritual crisis—either he must stand true to what he had come to believe these last few weeks and be blackballed by the religious order into which he had been born and raised or he must denounce them as the work of Satan. She would do anything in her power to keep him in the old system!

FRIDAY THE THIRTEENTH

The smells of early summer were in the air as Charlotte pulled the little red wagonload of firewood from the woodshed to the basement window, which had been modified to allow firewood to be passed through to feed the ravenous furnace in the cellar. Carl Jr. and Randy were getting to be good helpers, she thought, which was especially helpful now that the baby was ready to come any day. She hoped he would not arrive today. It was Friday the thirteenth, and the recent happenings in the little church still had her just a bit superstitious.

She thought back for the hundredth time to the Sunday evening service where it had all ended. Pastor Wally had not been there with his little family. She recalled seeing him walking slowly along the gravel road as they had passed on their way to the meeting. His shoulders were stooped, and his normally youthful, springy stride was replaced by an old man's shuffle. In the brief moment of eye contact, she saw that the usual enthusiastic sparkle had been extinguished, replaced by a flood of hurt and betrayal. She knew he would rebound, but it pricked her heart to see such a man bent and bowed.

The meeting had been simple but painful as one by one, the members stood to reaffirm their loyalty to the Mennonite faith and practices and denounce the incredible happenings of the past week as the work of Satan. She recalled watching the inner struggle rage in Carl. Although he had had misgivings about the increasingly bizarre events, it was still very difficult for him to call it the work of Satan. She felt his body tremble and saw the veins in his thick arms and neck bulge slightly as he stood to recite the required words through his clenched jaw. Then it was over, and they hadn't looked back. Pastor Wally's family had moved away, and the new interim pastor was doing well. But many would forever wonder what had really happened in the course of those few tumultuous weeks.

Suddenly, Charlotte was jerked back to the present as a terrible cramping pain nearly brought her to her knees. It was time; the little one wanted out!

When the pain passed, she sent Randy to "hurry and find daddy" and instructed Carl Jr. to throw the wagonload of wood into the cellar. Then, she waddled into the house to prepare for the thirty-mile trip to the nearest hospital in the city of Cedar Lake.

The labor was hard, and the little one came out crying and squiggling. When he was cleaned and attended, she cradled him for his first feeding. His little fists flailed, and he wailed indignantly, making her smile. "Ah yes," she murmured softly, "your daddy's temper!" Carl entered from the waiting room and looked down at the pair, his face suffused with satisfaction and pride. "Gonna hafta get a bigger farm with all these boys," he remarked.

As the summer unfolded, Charlotte began to feel she could live again. The awful fear she had lived with for those months was nearly gone now, at least for her. Little Michael was another matter. He was not a fussy baby by nature, but night after night, he would wake up crying and screaming. He was not hungry, and he didn't seem to be sick. In fact, all he required was for her to hold him close and coo or sing to him, and he would settle down and go back to sleep. A familiar dread began to nag at the back of her mind. She tried to push it away, but her heart already knew what her mind refused to accept; her terror had reached him in the womb, destroying the natural security a child finds in his mother. And he had been born on Friday, the thirteenth of May. She was not superstitious, but neither did this child need any more negative dynamics in his life!

Later that night, she lay in bed staring at the ceiling as Carl switched off the light and slid in beside her. It had been so long, she thought, since they had really touched hearts. She longed for the early days of their marriage when they would lay in each other's arms and talk into the wee hours of the morning. They just couldn't get enough of each other and wanted to know every little detail of each other's past. But it had all ended with the upheaval at the church.

She knew that deep down inside, Carl still believed that many of the events had been special blessings from God. As he struggled within his soul, he was becoming even less patient and more irritable. She was becoming alarmed at his rough treatment of the boys when his temper flared. He was losing his self-control. It bothered her when his whippings left marks on the tender bodies of the boys. Little Michael's nightly screams were irritating him, she realized, but so far, he hadn't struck him. It would be only a matter of time, she knew.

She wanted so badly to talk to him, to feel his strong arms around her, and to share heart to heart like they once had. She slowly turned toward him, hoping that he might be lying there with the same thoughts. Then, she was disappointed to hear his even breathing and soft snores. There would be no touching hearts tonight.

As the weeks turned to months, Carl's behavior became even more cold and distant. There were times when he would be in a good mood and talk, laugh, and joke with her or the boys. Her hopes would soar, only to be dashed to bits by a lightning-fast surge of uncontrolled fury when the smallest provocation enraged him. It seemed his whippings were becoming more about revenge than discipline.

Carl Jr. was becoming the primary focus of his abuse. Besides being the oldest, he was the most daring, and while it was difficult for her to admit, Charlotte was far more protective of her lovable little Randy.

One hard fact of life in the Raptor home was if you transgressed in any way and got caught, you would be whipped. There would be no opportunity to explain a situation that often was misunderstood in Carl's rush to judgment, which led to a nearly obsessive need to hurt the offending child. There was also no use in trying to apologize, no matter how heartfelt the apology was. All infractions must be answered by the hiss of a whip, a blow from the hand, or the more jarring but less painful kick to the buttocks. She cringed with shame and embarrassment as she remembered her recent trip to the doctor with Randy. He was having trouble shaking off flulike symptoms, and she had finally become worried enough to scrape together enough money to have him checked out. She remembered her horror when the doctor's eyes fell on Randy's bruised backside. It was covered with greenish purple bruises, some clearly showing the imprint of the hand that had beaten him.

The kindly doctor had stared into Charlotte's eyes, and she had wanted to sink through the floor of his cramped little office. Although in the future these defenseless little children would be protected by laws and social services, today, there was nothing he could do except to show his disapproval.

BIG TIMBER

"Mama," little Michael chirped. "I got a flower."

She smiled at the lively little boy, noting the light in his brown eyes. "That's nice," she said, giving the crumpled dandelion a quick perusal. He was such a sensitive child, she mused. It was odd though that a child so sensitive could so quickly erupt in angry outbursts. His older brothers had been quick to pick up on this and tormented him mercilessly. Carl, who was becoming less and less communicative, would not notice the teasing, but react violently to little Michael's outbursts. His spankings were becoming more brutal and would last until he had worked off his anger, at which point he would fling the child from him and stomp away. She noticed the boys were beginning to avoid him and shrink from physical contact with him. It was becoming more common to see marks on their little bodies from his abusive discipline. He was even becoming curt and rude to her. What was bothering him? She wondered if he was reacting to his own insecurities and weak emotional makeup. Their constant state of grinding poverty was also constantly working on his mind. Lately, he had been talking about getting a job in the big city of Rango, where his past experience as a mason would assure him a decent income. That would, however, necessitate Charlotte being alone in this hostile environment for weeks at a time. She was from hardy pioneer stock, but it was a lot to ask from a young mother with three small children and a small herd of cows to milk.

The farm was nestled in the heart of the enormous Big Timber Indian Reservation. The few Caucasian families in the community were a minority. The Indians tended to live in their rundown villages, but there were quite a few mixed-blood families living in shacks

22

scattered across the county. The village Indians tended to be heavy drinkers, as were the mixed-bloods. Their bouts of heavy drinking commonly led to serious accidents, vicious fights, and crime of every description. They relied heavily on thievery to support their drinking binges and supply fuel for their tattered vehicles, many of which sported no mufflers.

Tractors left setting overnight in the field would without fail be drained of gasoline by morning. Most of the people who had no garages would park their cars as close to their bedroom windows as possible so they could keep an eye out for gas thieves. By day, the thieves had a healthy respect for Carl's broad shoulders and thick arms, but at night, they would prowl his farm and buildings at will, looking for something to steal. Although constant vigilance needed to be exercised to protect property and thefts could be irritating, there was no prejudice against them as a people in the Raptor house or among the Mennonite people. The little mission church was there to help these once-proud people of the Chippewa nation, and most of them realized that their current condition was largely the result of government meddling and mismanagement.

*****

As the Raptors' financial situation worsened, it was becoming obvious that he would have to go elsewhere to seek employment.

"Everyone into the car," Carl ordered one evening. "We're going to Grandpa's tonight."

There was an immediate shout of joy from Carl Jr. and Randy. Little Michael caught the spirit and toddled to Charlotte. "Gampa?" he gurgled happily. Charlotte laughed and pulled him close as she climbed into the car with the rest.

The evening at Grandpa's was great fun as always. Grandpa was a short, jolly man with a balding head of thin gray hair and a spontaneous one-cackle laughter whenever something amused him. Grandma was also short and plump with a kind face and a heart full of love and tenderness for her family and especially her grandchildren. They had a cute, vivacious daughter Leona who was almost eight and had adopted a remarkably cute baby Indian boy "Rusty" who was nine. Grandma had gray eyes, which didn't quite fit her kindly face when she was upset; they could become hard and cold, much like her son Carl's eyes. But they were, as the Raptor boys would always agree, the perfect grandparents for little boys who lived on a mission station in the middle of a reservation full of rowdy Indians. They played table games, and Grandpa told a few funny stories, and the evening ended with some of grandma's tasty strawberry shortcake. Grandpa and Carl spent quite a bit of time talking in undertones, but Charlotte knew what the subject of their conversation was—going to Rango to find work. They would leave early Monday morning. She dreaded being alone in this harsh country with the small children, but there was no help for it she knew, they simply had to have the money!

The weekend was uneventful, boring the Raptor boys' thought. After the scary goings-on at the church, the services had become monotonous and ritualistic. The new pastor was a nice man, but didn't take the personal interest in people and children the way Pastor Wally had. Also, there was something just a bit odd about the way their parents related to him and his wife. They were friendly but cool, like the chill of a South Dakota autumn day when the sun was shining but couldn't quite warm the earth.

Randy heard the crunch of gravel under the Chevy's tires before dawn Monday morning. He didn't quite understand what was happening, but knew their daddy was leaving for a while, and it scared him.

Sliding out from under the warm blankets, he quietly crept across the room and looked out of the upstairs window overlooking the driveway. The moon was making its final descent in the night sky, and he could just make out the receding taillights of his father's car, blurred now by the cloud of dust rising behind it on the gravel road. His gaze shifted to the forest surrounding the farmhouse. It was a scary place for a small boy, a place to be entered only while clinging to the hand of his mother or father. As he watched, the mournful yipping howl of a coyote rose in the night air. It sent a shiver up his spine, and he scurried back to the safety of the blankets and the double bed he shared with Carl Jr.

The weeks and months passed quickly, with noticeably less tension in the home. Charlotte was a capable mother and farmer, and the boys felt secure in her care. She was good at hiding her own fears and insecurities and even found time to play with them after the day's work was done. She recognized the constant underlying fear in her youngest son and sought ways to help him overcome it, but it was deeply ingrained. Many nights, he woke up screaming in terror, and she would have to hold him close and comfort him back to sleep. A few times when Carl was home, she even asked him to help her pray over the trembling little form. She longed for him to find the peace she had found from the tormenting fear; but he was, she knew, too young to understand as she had that the nightmare was over.

He was growing into a lively little boy who was interested in everything around him. He was especially fascinated by the bunk beds where Randy and Carl Jr. slept. It had been a custom-made gift from Charlotte's father, and Michael was intrigued by the varnished pine finish and little ladder up to the top bunk. He had learned the hard way to respect the parameters of the top bunk, after he had been playing up there and tumbled over the edge, landing on his head. His ear-splitting screams brought his mother running, but he seemed to be more frightened than in pain. It seemed, Charlotte mused, that this child had to learn all of life's hard lessons by painful experience. Was that the reasons for the repeated nightmares he suffered from? They seemed to be coming more frequently now, and she was afraid Carl's patience was running thin from being awakened so many nights by the boy's frightened cries. She desperately hoped he would not start whipping the boy for this too. She believed that they shared the guilt for the child's fear. She thought back to the weeks of black fear and despair she had endured while the baby was forming in her womb. How could it have not affected him?

GREEN BEANS, WEEDS, AND THE THING

The shadows from behind the house were just beginning to touch the rusty old rain barrel under the sagging gutter spout. Three little faces were pressed against the pane of the living room window as eager eyes scanned the road, looking for the cloud of dust that would accompany their daddy's car returning from two weeks of work in Rango.

"There he comes!" yelled Randy. "Daddy's home!"

Their finances had greatly improved over the months since Carl had been working in Rango. But there was always a greater sense of security when he was back home.

After supper, Carl retrieved a brown paper bag he had brought home with him and set it on the table. Three excited pairs of eyes watched as he slowly and dramatically drew out the present for them. They stared at it dumbfounded. Finally, Carl Jr. found his voice. "What *is* it?" he asked. "It's not a car, and it's not a pickup, but it looks like both!"

"It's called an El Camino," Carl explained. "The car companies combined a car and pickup design to make these. This is a toy just like the real ones."

"Well, there sure is a lot of cool stuff in the big city!" Randy commented.

"Yes," Carl replied. "But it all costs a lot of money."

As Michael drifted off to sleep that night, he thought that when he grew up, he would live in the big city and have lots of money so he could buy all that cool stuff.

The thing came for him again that night. First, he was standing alone in a dark forest. Then, a low and spooky moaning sound built into a thunderous raging howl! The treetops began to sway wildly; then, they turned into a swirling, living black red and green monstrosity that reached hungrily for him! He had to run! He must flee, but he couldn't move, and it was on him, swirling around him and wrapping him up to swallow him alive. He was too terrified to move or even scream. A choked, gasping gurgle came from his throat as he tried to breathe through his terror. Finally, he found his voice. "No!" he screamed. "Go away. Let me go!" It continued to wrap him, tighter and tighter. He began to fight it with every ounce of strength in his small body, kicking and struggling, but it was no use. He was losing the battle.

"Michael, Michael, it's okay. It's just a dream. I have you now. Wake up," Charlotte's voice slowly penetrated his terrified consciousness. The pressure of the black thing wrapped around him gradually came into his focus as his mother's arms. He lay there crying and trembling violently, his normally tanned face white with fear. When he was fully awake, she spoke quietly and soothingly to him. "It's just a bad dream," she told him. "It won't come back again tonight." She tucked him back under the covers and softly sang a soothing little song for him. He tried to be brave for her sake as she turned out the light and left the room. What was this thing? What did it want from him? Would it one day eat him alive, and then, he would be dead? Slowly, he drifted off to a dreamless sleep.

Saturday morning dawned clear and cool. Michael woke to the sound of someone hammering on metal out in the old garage across the drive from the house. He slid to the cold hardwood floor and quickly pulled on his T-shirt and cutoff pants. He was often the first one out of bed in the morning, but today, his daddy was home, and nobody ever beat daddy out of bed.

Carl was mounting tires on an axle salvaged from an old Ford Model T. He was surrounded by an assortment of parts. Michael saw an old bus seat and two long slender poles among the parts. "What are you making?" he asked when he could no longer contain his curiosity. "Something to make little boys ask questions," Carl replied with a twinkle in his eyes. Michael watched with silent admiration. Although he feared Carl, he also hero-worshipped him. Carl was well known in the community as the man who could make anything he needed out of whatever he had. Despite his volatile temper, most of the time, he was good to his wife and children and would find and repair or even make toys for them. His most impressive toy had been a large pedal car. It was big enough for a medium-sized child to sit in and had a functional steering wheel and pedals to propel it. Carl had tinkered with the pedal drive system and gotten it functioning like new. Carl Jr. called it the "Daddy Do," and the name stuck. In fact, it stuck so well that years later, Charlotte would have to explain to the younger boys that the car was not actually manufactured under the name "Daddy Do."

"Are you gonna ride Patsy today?" Michael asked.

Patsy was the beautiful bay filly Carl had raised and trained to ride. He would sit the boys on her back and lead her around the pasture. Carl Jr. could ride her by himself, and Randy was riding her around the pasture, but had not tried riding her on the road yet. Michael squeezed his eyes shut tightly and imagined himself high on the horse's back, looking down on Carl's wavy brown hair as he led the horse. He always felt like a king on top of the world, surveying his kingdom at those times.

"I suppose we might find time to do that if you boys have all been good while I was gone," Carl teased. Michael looked up at him, his brown eyes serious and a bit anxious. "I only got three spankings," he said. "Is that good enough?"

"I suppose it is," Carl chuckled. "Let's see how the day goes."

Michael drifted out of the garage, drawn as usual to the horse pasture. He could spend hours watching the horses munch the green grass and romp in the field. Patsy was his favorite, perhaps because he sensed how special she was to his daddy. He was always impressed when Carl would saddle her up and swing up on her back and thunder off to move the half-wild cattle to another pasture. He would squeeze his eyes shut and imagine it was him riding tall in the saddle, looking down on the world as it swept past under Patsy's thundering hooves. Oh yes, he thought. Someday, it would be him!

There was little time that day to further contemplate Carl's noisy project in the garage as today was weeding day. Weeding day was a day the boys thoroughly detested, and it came several times each week. Charlotte kept a huge garden and had a passion against weeds. Her three tykes would be sent there for hours at a time to pull weeds, a job each of them hated with every fiber of their beings. When possible, Charlotte would bring her hoe and assist with the weeding, but rather than appreciate the help, her small sons would envy her hi-tech method of weed removal.

"She doesn't even have to bend over like we do," Carl Jr. would grumble.

Randy, always mama's boy, would usually jump to her defense. "We can't use a hoe because we would chop out good plants," he said defensively.

"That's baloney!" Carl Jr. snapped. "She just wants us to have to work harder!"

"Yes," said Michael decisively. "Baloney!"

Although he didn't totally understand the argument, he was less than two years younger than Randy, and Carl Jr.'s opinion was always more authoritative to him than Randy's.

They bent their backs again to the task of pulling weeds. Soon, however, their attention was drawn to a big shiny automobile cruising slowly up the gravel road toward their farm. As they watched, it turned into their drive and crawled up the lane past the garden. It stopped beside the garden, and a rather distinguished-looking gentleman got out and walked through the garden gate. He was looking closely at the long rows of string beans. The boys watched nervously as he bent down for close examination.

"Can I help you?" Charlotte's voice from beyond the gate seemed to have a slight edge. This garden was her pride and joy, as well as her enormous contribution to the family's survival. She and Carl had carefully cultivated it, fertilized it each year with manure from the cow barn, and surrounded it with a neat, tight fence to keep out all the wild forest critters. Each year, Charlotte would sell some of the extra fresh produce to summer vacationers at the nearby resorts. It was a source of welcome cash, which always seemed to be in short supply in the Raptor household.

"I came to buy some string beans," the man announced.

"Sorry," Charlotte shook her head. "They aren't ready to pick yet."

"They look ready to me," the man replied.

Charlotte's voice took on an even sharper edge. This was her kingdom, and she was feeling invaded. "They will be ready next week. You can come back then."

"I won't be here next week, and they are ready now!" the man responded, looking annoyed.

Charlotte's slight frame stiffened, and her brown eyes grew hard. "This is my garden, and I decide when to pick what in here," she said icily. "I think you had better leave now!"

The boys watched in amazement as the "rich man" walked dejectedly to his car and drove away. This was a side to their mother that they rarely saw, and they were mightily impressed.

Charlotte's eyes softened as she surveyed her three little helpers.

"You are doing well boys. Finish your rows, and you can stop for today."

She turned and walked back to the wash line where she had been hanging out laundry, every inch the queen of her own little estate. *The beans could be picked any day now*, she mused.

Bunny Boots and Labradors

Carl Jr. and Randy stared out the living room window at the blowing and drifting snow. It was another northern winter blizzard, and it was going into its third day with no letup. The whole family had been confined to the house except for chores and the absolute essentials. Charlotte had brought out the chipped porcelain chamber pot for their bathroom needs instead of risking the children getting lost in the swirling whiteness on their way to the outhouse. It had been fun for them all at first, eating popcorn, playing games, and listening to Charlotte read stories.

But now, the firewood supply in the basement was perilously low, and Carl was getting worried. He usually kept about a week's supply of firewood in the cellar to supply the ravenous monster of a furnace, and he had been thinking that it was about time to resupply it when this blizzard had come howling in. If it didn't let up by tomorrow, he would need to venture out to find more firewood.

The morning dawned crystal clear and bitterly cold. Michael, always an early riser, made his way down the icy cold hardwood stairs to the living room where Carl and Charlotte were enjoying their morning cup of coffee.

"As soon as chores are finished, we need to make some firewood," Carl was saying.

"Take the boys with you," Charlotte said. "They need to work off some energy!"

After breakfast, the eager boys bundled up in their thick parkas with the fur-lined hoods. "Can I wear the Bunny Boots?" Carl Jr. asked.

"Go ahead," Charlotte responded. "But you know they are kinda big for you."

Carl Jr. went out to the icy cold porch and came back holding the Bunny Boots. They were clumsy, odd-looking bulbous creations, covered with white fur like a snowshoe rabbit, and sported hardwood soles that had absolutely no traction on ice or packed snow.

Carl had found several pairs of them at the army surplus store where he had been told the boots were Swedish army issue. They had been the cause of many embarrassing and sometimes painful falls for Carl Jr., but he was starting to get the hang of how to use them.

The positive thing about the boots was that they were always warm and would rarely, if ever, allow your feet to get wet. If you could stay upright, they were the perfect footwear for these bitterly cold northern winters.

The arctic air bit their faces the instant they stepped out the front porch door. The boys gazed around them in awe at the huge drifts. The swirling snow had drifted against the two-story garage and was piled up as high as the roof. The driveway was drifted shut with snow piled higher than the family car in several places.

Suddenly, there was a sound of barking as Sporty, the neighbor's huge black Labrador dog, bounded toward them. Michael shrank back in fear. Sporty was bigger than him and had a deep-throated bark that sounded to him more like an angry roar. He was rather bad-tempered and had bitten the boys several times for reasons only his canine brain could fathom.

Randy stretched out his arm and called the big lab to him. Sporty came willingly, and Randy petted him and scratched behind his ears. Michael watched, impressed by Randy's courage in the face of what was to him such obvious danger!

They started down the hill toward the barn where Carl was harnessing the horses to the bobsled. The sled was a very common type used extensively by loggers. The undercarriage consisted of two pairs of very strong runners, one pair trailing the other, connected by crossed log chains. Above each pair of runners was a huge oak crossbeam, and usually, there would be heavy oak planks spanning the beams to create a bed for carrying cargo.

The boys heard the jingle of harness chains as they rounded the corner of the barn and saw Carl in the finishing stages of hitching the team of draft horses to the sled. They clambered onto the sled, and Carl started the horses with a clicking sound from his tongue.

The drifts deepened as they neared the timber line. Soon, the horses could no longer walk through the drifts and resorted to lunging bounds, which jerked the sleigh. The boys hung on for dear life, and Carl Jr. clutched the "Swede saw," a hand-operated saw made with a half hoop of aluminum tubing with a wickedly sharp and aggressive cutting blade strung between the open ends.

They reached the woods, and Carl and Carl Jr. began to cut dead trees with the Swede saw while Randy gathered smaller branches. Michael was of little use; it was all he could do to propel himself through the snow.

When the bobsled was half loaded, Carl decided it was enough for the team to pull through the deep snow, and everyone climbed onto the logs, and they headed back to the house.

Carl unhitched the team and left the loaded sled stand by the "firewood window" in the basement and then headed for the barn followed by Carl Jr. and Randy. Michael was busy exploring the underside of the bobsled and admiring the load of wood, which to him was huge.

Charlotte was busy with her laundry in the frigid front porch. She felt a sense of relief that the storm was over and life could get back to normal. As she reflected on the bitter winter and ferocious blizzards that were such a part of life here, she heard what sounded like muffled screams from a child. She paused and cocked her head to listen—nothing.

She resumed her washing, swishing the clothes around in the galvanized washtub. There it was again, louder this time. Quickly, she slipped on her parka and boots and went outside to investigate.

She rounded the corner of the house to where the new load of firewood stood and screamed in horror. The big black Labrador was dragging Michael face down in the snow, his teeth firmly clamped on the furry bill of his winter cap. The cap had a chin strap that was snapped securely under the small boy's chin, making him helpless to escape. The fresh snow was muffling his screams, which were cut short each time the dog dragged him again, choking his air supply.

Desperately, Charlotte looked around for a weapon and spied the load of firewood. She seized a large stick and went after the big dog. He saw her coming, let go of the cap, and scrambled away.

Charlotte picked up the terrified, half-frozen child and carried him into the house. She set him over the register above the furnace and removed his outer clothes, rubbing his limbs and reassuring him that he was okay now.

Just what he needs, she thought, *something else to fear!* While he suffered no serious injury from the experience, Michael would carry an innate fear of dogs all through life, even though he would come to love them. His life would be a roller coaster of fearing that which he loved.

The bitter cold days of winter finally gave way to the fresh warmth of spring. The huge drifts and banks of snow began to melt rapidly, flooding the lawn and driveway. One morning, they awoke to the sound of rain drumming on the roof. It rained hard all day and most of the night. By morning, there was water everywhere, more than a foot deep in places. After breakfast, Michael was staring out the window when he saw Carl Jr. go sailing past, literally. He had emptied a rain barrel and, using a pole for guidance, was floating around the lawn in it. Soon, Randy located a stock tank for himself and Michael, and they embarked on their own luxury cruise. It was high adventure, and they floated between the trees in the woods, around the evergreen trees, and through the huge lilac bushes. They had never realized that boating could be this much fun.

"Hey guys," Carl Jr. said as he floated past. "We ought to get us a real boat. This is a blast!"

All too soon however, their little crafts began to scrape and run aground as the floodwaters receded. The disappointed little sailors returned their crafts to their former locations and set off in search of other adventures.

THE CATTLE PROD

Fall had come to the swamps and forests of the Big Timber Indian Reservation. Five-year-old Michael was in his glory, chasing the brightly colored leaves as the brisk fall breezes skipped them across the lawn and into the surrounding forests. *It's strange*, Charlotte thought, *how a little tyke so lively and determined could be so passionate about flowers and pretty leaves.* "The Lord God made them all," she mused, thinking of a refrain from the little chorus the children often sang in Sunday school. A shadow flickered across her face as she thought of the child's tormented nights. "Please God," she breathed. "Take it away! Let him be a normal child!"

*****

"Hey guys, look what I brought." Carl Jr. held up a book of matches triumphantly. "We can make us a fire!"

"Are you sure we should?" Seven-year-old Randy asked nervously. "Mommy might not like it."

"She can't see it," Carl Jr. replied, surveying the thick foliage around them. "Come on, get some sticks."

Fifteen minutes later, the three boys were huddled around a small crackling fire.

"We should bring some marshmallows sometime," Carl Jr. remarked.

Randy said nothing, still wrestling with his troubled conscience. It was fun, he had to admit, but what if they got caught?

Soon, it was time to go back to the house, and they carefully extinguished the fire and covered the ashes with dirt. This would be the first of many such fires they would enjoy without their parents' knowledge, but the edge of forbidden excitement would never again be quite as keen as it had been today!

They returned to the house to find Carl in an ugly mood. A cow had died, and another was sick, and his paycheck from Rango had been less than expected. He could turn from happy to furious almost instantly, and the boys immediately realized that the supper table tonight would be a good place to be seen and not heard.

The silence seemed to increase the tension, and as soon as the meal was finished, Carl curtly ordered the boys to the barn to begin chores. Carl and Charlotte went to the living room to talk over a cup of coffee. They were having a serious disagreement, and both of their tempers were rising.

Soon, they were shouting at each other; then, there was the *slap* of Carl's hand striking his wife. The instant he struck her, he knew he had crossed a very dangerous line! The house went absolutely silent for several interminable moments.

Finally, Carl found the courage to look at his wife. Her dark eyes were aflame with fury, but her voice was as cold as the wind that carried the northern winter blizzards!

"Carl," she said with a deadly calmness. "I married you because I loved you, and I still do. But lately, you have become someone I hardly know. Now, know this—if you *ever* hit me again, I *will* leave you, and if I do, you will *never* be a part of my life again!"

Carl's shoulders slumped, and the fire of fury left his eyes, replaced by a look of defeat. He would never again take his anger and frustration out on Charlotte; his small, defenseless sons would now bear it all. The boys were also too young to understand that Carl's frustration would only be increased by having been withstood, and he would seem almost to have an extra need to bully those still within his power.

Silently, the defeated man exited the house and headed for the barn. He sent Michael into the house to assist with the dishwashing.

Sometime later, Charlotte appeared in the kitchen, and the dishes were finished in silence. When the last plate and drinking glass were properly stored in the battered old kitchen cabinet, they walked together out into the gathering dusk.

They strolled across the lawn to the flower garden. Michael as always was soon burying his face in the fading roses and mums. Charlotte sat on the stump of an old maple tree Carl had cut down the preceding year. Her mind was still reeling from the emotional trauma of the incident with Carl.

She had also recently become aware that another child was growing in her womb—another doctor bill and another mouth to feed and diapers to wash—and they could barely make ends meet now. Silently, she bowed her head to pray, pleading to the God she knew was there to help them survive in this harsh land.

*****

On his next trip back from Rango, Carl produced another wonder, but this time, it was not a toy. It resembled a large, long-handled flashlight; but instead of a glass and bulb at the head, two metal prongs protruded about an inch apart. Charlotte immediately recognized it and a look of disapproval clouded her face.

"What do you need a cattle prod for?" she asked apprehensively.

"Why to control uncooperative horses and cattle," he replied nonchalantly. "They really put out an electric jolt!"

To illustrate his point, he held the steel blade of his knife against one of the metal probes and allowing a quarter-inch gap between the blade and the other probe. When he hit the switch, there was an angry hissing, frying sound, and a visible blue flame danced between the probe and his knife blade. The arcing flame and the vicious sizzling sound made Michael shudder. He felt sorry for any animal his father used that thing on, even if they were big and strong.

Somehow, Carl found lots of animals that "needed" the electric prod used on them. But Michael noticed that he never used it on his beloved horses. He didn't need to ask why, even if he had dared to ask. Carl loved horses almost more than he loved people, and although he was not above punishing them into submission, he was never abusive to them. Michael once saw him give Uncle Rusty a serious thrashing for slashing a draft horse with the driving lines just to see the marks it left on the horse's broad rump where the dust had been displaced by the blows. No, the horses just didn't seem to need the electric jolts.

But the little boys did! Carl Jr. was the first to feel it. He managed to anger his father during chores one night, and Carl seized the prod from its nail on the wall and gave him a short jolt through the seat of his trousers. Carl Jr. shrieked like he had been scalded and raced out the barn door and into the evening shadows.

Late one afternoon several weeks later, Michael failed to show up in the barn in time to begin his chores. He had gotten sidetracked in the house where he was lying on his stomach on the dining room floor and talking through the heat register to the basement. It made a hollow echo that the boys found amusing, and Michael was laughing when he heard the ominous sound of Carl's boots stomping in through the porch directly toward him. He was halfway to his feet when his father's arm snaked out and grabbed his upper arm, twisting him around to stare up into his father's furious glare! The cold fury in those gray eyes always terrified him, even when the anger wasn't directed toward him. But this time, it was all about him and his rotten irresponsibility toward his chores. His stomach churned as he realized that he was in for a serious whipping again!

But he was mistaken. There would be no whipping today. Carl half dragged him into the barn and then dramatically reached for the awful cattle prod on the wall. He jammed it against the seat of Michael's trousers and gave him a three-second jolt of high-voltage electric. The prod spat enough voltage to make a thousand-pound steer bellow, and the effect on a forty-pound boy was devastating. Michael screamed as the voltage surged through his small body! It was like being burned, beaten, and cut all at the same time. Fortunately, his father managed to control his anger enough to limit it to one jolt. He threw his rejected son to the ground where he lay sobbing from the burning pain spreading from his buttocks through his whole body. He would never in his lifetime forget that torturous jolt from the awful instrument!

LADDIE

Michael sat on the stump of a fallen tree at the edge of the lawn and surveyed the property absently. The gray stucco house was a sturdy two-story building sitting atop a knoll. Down the hill was the barn, a crude, unpainted wooden structure for the farm animals. The horses would often seek shelter from storms in the surrounding forest rather than the ramshackle structure. The gravel road ran past the barnyard and curved uphill into the woodland north of the house. A long gravel driveway ascended through the stand of timber toward the house. The driveway was bordered on the west by the huge, fenced garden and finally curved around the house and ended at the large two-story garage built from rough-sawn native lumber and covered with tar paper held in place with plaster laths.

The garage was a spooky place to Michael and his brothers. They always suspected that the Indians skulked in there at night and thought they heard strange noises and saw shadowy forms around the entrance. One evening during chores, Carl ordered Michael to retrieve a rope he had left upstairs in the barn. Michael's heart sank to his toes. But he knew better than to argue with his father, so calling Laddie to accompany him, he climbed the hill and entered the spooky garage. The inside was so dark he could hardly see the steps leading upstairs where, without a doubt, he was about to lose his life horribly at the hands of a very bad man or wild animal! As his trembling legs slowly carried him up the stairs to his doom, he began to speak to Laddie in a voice designed to reach whoever was up there.

"Laddie"—he said—"you sure are a big strong dog. Mean too! Why those sharp teeth of yours could rip somebody to pieces in no time!"

His effort at mind control was not terribly effective, so he made a final rush up the last few steps, seized the rope, and raced back down the stairs and out the door to safety. Laddie romped comfortably behind him, completely oblivious to the miracle that they had made it out alive.

Making matters worse for the boys was the fact that the little wooden outhouse was now located directly behind the garage. It had previously been located in a small stand of aspens near the garden, but as always, the hole beneath it filled with waste, and the structure had to be placed over a new hole. The old location was now a lovely flower garden.

The new location was not terribly spooky by day, but the boys were deathly afraid of making the hundred-yard trek there by night. The path led directly past the doorway of the spooky garage and the shadowy trees opposite the doorway. The boys would always beg each other to accompany them when a nocturnal visit was unavoidable. First though, they would wrestle mightily with nature's call in a usually vain attempt to hold out until morning.

Daytime visits, however, presented their own frightening risks. Bees! The boys had been stung often enough by the vicious little insects to have a deep fear of them and would go to ridiculous lengths to avoid getting near enough to get stung! The problem was the bees liked to buzz and swarm in and around the toilet seat holes and found the little bare bottoms an irresistible repository for their nasty little stingers.

For the boys, the obvious solution to this problem was to leave their deposits elsewhere. The surrounding woods and bushes carried the risk of encounters with snakes or poison ivy. The well-worn dirt path was the safest option, but picking it up and throwing it into the bushes was so distasteful.

Their dilemma was solved by Laddie, the faithful family canine. Laddie loved to supplement his diet of squirrel and carrion with their droppings. All that was needed was to whistle him up on the way to the outhouse. They could poop right on the path, and he would always happily take care of cleanup detail. He was the perfect multi-purpose canine!

Michael turned his gaze back to the road. Any time now, mommy would be home. She had been sick, and daddy had taken her to the hospital, and Michael was worried and scared without her. Carl had been unusually kind to the boys though in her absence.

As his gaze searched the road again, he thought he saw a small cloud of dust in the distance. He watched it grow larger until the hazy form of the family Chevy emerged. He shouted for his brothers and raced to meet the car as it ascended the drive and rounded the curve to come to a stop in front of the house.

Michael ran to the passenger door and with both hands managed to pull it open. Charlotte looked pale and thinner but smiled at him and climbed out of the car, holding a blanked-wrapped bundle. As the three boys crowded around, she lowered the bundle for them to see.

Michael found himself looking into the unblinking eyes of a tiny baby boy. "This is your new brother Johnny," she said. Michael was fascinated. Where had she found him? "Mommy, did you buy him in town?" he asked perplexed. "Not really," she replied. "I brought him from the hospital."

It didn't make sense to Michael that the hospital would give out babies, but he would think more about that another time. He noticed the horses standing around the huge cast-iron water tank and went over to pet them. Patsy's coat was soft and warm, and he told her all about the new baby as he stroked her silky coat. Then, he stroked each of the big draft horses in turn and finally joined his brothers on their trek down the hill to the barn for their evening chores.

"Michael, wake up," Randy was shaking him awake from his afternoon nap. "Grandpas are here."

Sleepily, Michael slid out of bed and followed Randy downstairs to where Grandma was cooing over baby Johnny. His Aunt Leona who was quite a little mother at twelve was begging for her turn to hold him. Leona was cute and vivacious, with a streak of tomboy that kept her abreast of anything her older brother and small nephews could devise. She rode horses, played ball, and fished as well as any of them.

As they clustered around Grandma and little Johnny, the rumble of a large truck coming up the drive drew their attention. "There's the truck," Leona announced.

Michael was confused. Trucks were rare on this farm. "Why is the truck here?" he asked, a feeling of foreboding knotting his stomach.

"To get Patsy," Leona replied. "Your daddy sold her to pay for the baby bill."

Michael stared at her in shock and disbelief! His daddy would never sell Patsy! She was the finest horse he had ever owned, born right here on the farm, and carefully trained to saddle and harness. Selling her would be like selling one of the family!

"Patsy's not-so old," his voice caught in his throat choking on the terrible word.

Leona, oblivious to his horror, tried to be funny. "No, she's not so old, but she *is* sold," she said authoritatively. Michael turned away, trying to control the pounding in his head and choking back his tears. His legs felt wooden as he stumbled out the door to see Carl leading Patsy up the long loading ramp into the truck. He saw the special bond between man and horse as Carl put one arm around the mare's neck and gently caressed her for the last time with the other. He saw Carl murmur something into her ear and then turned and walked down the ramp. A tear glistened on his weather-beaten face, and he flicked it away. Life was hard here in this land of forests and Indians. A man did what a man had to do.

The sun was high in the sky the next morning when Michael sleepily descended the stairs and entered the kitchen. Randy was on his knees on the cupboard below the kitchen window, and Charlotte was standing beside him. Both were looking out the window and laughing uproariously. His curiosity aroused, Michael climbed up beside Randy and looked out.

Carl was trying to move the heifers using one of the young draft horses for a saddle horse. It hadn't taken the fleet-footed heifers long to discover that they could outrun the horse, and they were having the time of their lives. Carl was trying to keep them bunched on the road, but as soon as he headed off the escape attempt of one, two more would raise their tails skyward and make a break for the timber.

He needs Patsy, Michael thought, and a wave of sadness washed over him as he thought of how he and Carl would both miss her. Would he ever see her again?

*****

It was Sunday again. Sundays meant church for the Raptor family. Skipping church for any reason except serious illness simply didn't happen. Michael liked some things about church and disliked others. He always looked forward to being with his best friend Dode. Dode was Pastor Oliver's son, Doyle, who was his age and shared nearly all of his interests and passions. There were other friends as well, and they all played together afterward.

He usually liked the Sunday school hour, depending on who the teacher was. But the sermons were something to be endured. They tended to be long and tedious monologues on whatever subject the pastor chose to bore them with. Sometimes, his parents allowed him to sit with Dode during the sermon, but usually, they didn't want to complicate their lives by having to monitor his behavior across the aisle, thus compromising their intense focus on the uninteresting exegesis from the podium.

Today, their Sunday school class teacher was Grandma Raptor. Michael liked when Grandma taught; she could make the dusty old Bible stories come alive and make the stuffy characters seem almost real! Today, though, she was telling about the crucifixion of Jesus and making it so real that it might have happened last week. She explained how after doing good and kind things His whole life, His enemies had finally caught up with Him and were whipping and torturing Him all night long. Her description of the beatings made a dramatic firsthand impression on Michael, how well he could relate to that! Then Grandma commented, "Unless you repent of your sins and accept Jesus's sacrifice to cleanse your life, you are as guilty as anyone in that mob who killed Him!"

Michael was trying to figure out why that would be so, but his attention was soon drawn to another point she was making. She was explaining what great and enduring love God had for His children, so much so that He would let evil mankind torture and kill His own son so His children could have a way back to Him.

"God's love for you is just like your father's love," she said. "And He loves you just like your father does!"

Michael felt suddenly deflated. God loved him the way his father did? Then He didn't love Michael Raptor at all! He had never really felt love from his father, only anger and even hatred. He was only another burden his father had to bear, another care when he could barely handle life as it was! He would never in his life remember his father looking him in the face and saying the three magic words, *I love you*. No, Michael was sure God loved people like Grandma had said. The problem was one little boy named Michael was not lovable to a father, in heaven or on earth.

HORSES AND GOPHER PAWS

"Get ready, Laddie!" Carl Jr. told the salivating collie, as he grasped the sapling. The boys had found a new sport to brighten their days after discovering the lightning-fast reflexes of their dog. They would tree a squirrel in a sapling and shake it out of the tree for the young dog. Laddie would nearly always grab the squirming squirrel the instant it hit the ground. Often, he would even catch it in midair. His speed and reflexes never failed to amaze the boys.

In years to come, taking the life of an animal would become distasteful to them, but here on the reservation where buying food used up precious cash, hunting and butchering was a way of life.

The plump red squirrel was hanging on for dear life, and Carl Jr.'s shakes were failing to dislodge it, so Randy joined the effort. A few vigorous shakes later, the squirrel lost its grip and sailed toward the ground. Laddie was waiting, his entire body quivering with anticipation.

As the squirrel neared the ground, Laddie sprang upward in a graceful arc that perfectly intersected the downward course of the squirrel. There was a squeak and a snap of teeth, and it was over. The squirrel never touched the ground; and today, Laddie, who would never in his life taste dog food, would eat well.

This sport of hunting to supplement Laddie's diet would go on for years. Laddie had become a constant companion of the boys, even following them on their horseback excursions. It seemed he never tired.

"Let's go for a horse ride," Michael suggested.

Randy and Carl Jr. considered the suggestion. Carl Jr. now had his own horse, a two-year-old filly who was half saddle and half draft horse. He had mostly broken her to ride himself, and he was becoming a fine horseman.

Although all the older Raptor boys would become daredevils in their own right, Carl Jr. would always be the one who lived "closest to the edge." He seemed to have courage beyond his sense of self-preservation.

Now, he mentally weighed the pros and cons of a horseback ride. He would like to work with his filly some more, but Michael was just learning to ride by himself, and daddy had restricted him to a tame old draft horse who couldn't keep up to the speed he and Randy liked to ride.

"Okay," he decreed. "We'll go riding if Michael doesn't complain if he gets left behind."

"I won't," Michael promised, eager at the thought of sitting atop eight hundred pounds of horseflesh and feeling the muscles rippling under him.

They made their way to the barn for a bucket of grain. Their horses were never tame enough to catch unless the boys lured them with a bucket of grain. Today, they were extra spooked, and even the grain bucket failed to entice them. Carl Jr. was fast losing what little patience he possessed as the skittish horse herd bolted from one end of the large pasture to the other.

Finally, he opened the barn door and called for the collie. "Sic 'em, Laddie!" he shouted as the herd bolted again.

The dog needed no encouragement and was after the herd in a flash. The horses saw him coming and redoubled their speed. The ground shook beneath their hooves as they thundered around the huge pasture.

The light brown form of the pursuing collie was a blur as he closed the distance. The horses were running for their lives, with a generations-old fear of pursuing wolves, and the collie was closing in.

The boys watched with silent fascination as the collie's bounds brought her within striking distance of the mare in the rear of the herd. With a magnificent leap, Laddie caught the mare and clamped his mouth over the end of her streaming tail.

The mare screamed and rolled her eyes in terror. She rounded the corner of the pasture and thundered toward the barn. Laddie lost his footing as she rounded the turn and soared through the air, his mouth still firmly clamped on the tail.

The boys began to laugh at the drama unfolding before their eyes. The horses, though, had had enough. They raced for the relative safety of the open barn door. And with his usual split-second timing, Laddie released the tail and came to a dramatic, sliding stop as the mare streaked through the door.

His eyes were agleam and his mouth open with what the boys were sure was a smile of victory. He had done it, and what a thrill it had been!

Randy quickly slammed the barn door shut and then turned to praise the grinning dog. They entered the barn full of excited, milling horses, and after each boy selected his mount, the rest of the herd was let out to pasture again. Fifteen minutes later, they were galloping down the road. The horses' hooves raised little puffs of dust on the dry gravel. They usually only had two speeds at which they rode, either a full gallop or a walk to allow the horses to catch their breath.

They headed east toward the little county store across from the one-room county school. Each of them had gopher paws to cash in at Hank Keefer's store.

Gopher paws were one of the few ways the boys could raise a bit of money in this cash-starved county. The government had placed a bounty on pocket gophers, which were a plague to the fields and pastures. The little rodents would make huge networks of underground tunnels with occasional mounds where the tunnels would Y off into a third tunnel. Each of these junctions would be marked by a mound of soft, fluffy topsoil.

The Raptor boys had acquired spring-loaded gopher traps, and Grandpa Raptor had taught them how to dig down under the dirt mounds and set the traps directly in the junction. Each trap was connected to a light chain with a loop at the end that would be anchored to a wooden stake aboveground. The hole would then be covered with a board and the mound of dirt replaced over it. The front feet would be removed from the dead gopher, and each pair could be turned in at the Keefer's corner store for two cents bounty.

The boys brought their horses to a stop in front of the store, dismounted, and tied them to the huge pines shading the entrance. Then, they strolled past the ancient gas pump in front of the ramshackle building, and Carl Jr. reached for the handle of the sagging screen door in front.

From inside the store, a chorus of raucous barking and snarls erupted.

Michael shrank behind Randy in fear. He would always be terrified of the mean-spirited dogs that were the only family Hank could claim. A jangle of sleigh bells attached by a cord to the door announced their entry.

The rough, unfinished floorboards creaked as Carl Jr. strode confidently to the sagging sales counter and opened the paper bag containing his gopher paws. Hank Keefer was a tall, rawboned man who must have been born old since no one in the community ever remembered him being anything else. His corner store was more of a shack, located at the junction of two gravel roads. His building was low and crudely constructed, with a few small windows usually covered with dust and grime. The interior was also crude and dingy, with a disorganized sales counter running down the center of the room nearly to the end wall. He now counted the shriveled paws proffered by Carl Jr. and then, without a word, opened the battered tin cash register and dug out twelve pennies. Carl Jr. juggled the pennies from hand to hand as he perused the enticing display of candy jars.

As he was making his choice, Randy and Michael cashed in their paws and began making their decisions. This was the only shopping they would ever know until they were teenagers, but no millionaire ever enjoyed his money more! It never crossed their minds that it might have been a good idea for Hank to have washed his hands between the acts of handling the dead gophers' feet and handing them their unwrapped candy.

Their shopping complete, they exited the store and sat on the rickety wooden bench out front. They munched happily on their purchases, each with a five-cent bottle of Coca-Cola close at hand. As they relaxed, they watched their horses switch their tails at the pesky flies. Michael was fascinated by the way horses could twitch their skin wherever the swishing tails couldn't reach to keep the irritating flies away. Diagonally across the four-way gravel intersection stood the tiny white clapboard schoolhouse. It stood in the outer corner of approximately one acre of ground where the area pioneers had cleared back the thick forest and built it with the native lumber, strong backs, and their work-roughened hands. The perimeter of the surrounding forest was dark and brooding, even sinister to a small boy who fought a constant battle with fears.

WELFARE KID

Thirty minutes later, they were mounted and headed back to the farm. It was racing time, and the horses sensed it. Perched up on the clumsy draft mare, Michael's blood was pounding in his ears! He knew that the older boys would leave him eating their dust in the first spurt, but for those few seconds, he would be in the race!

He glanced at Randy and Carl Jr. Neither of them was talking, but their horses felt their tension and began to prance and tug at the bits. Carl Jr. who was slightly behind Randy edged his dancing filly even with Randy's and suddenly dug his heels into his filly's ribs and yelled, "Heeeeyaaaah!"

Randy was ready for him, and his shout matched Carl Jr.'s. Huge clods of dirt spurted from their horses' hooves as they instantly sprang from a prancing walk into a full gallop. Michael who had tried to be ready for this was soon dodging the flying clods and stones thrown up by the faster horses' hooves. His little hand was flailing the old mare furiously to little advantage. He was still several hundred yards behind when he saw the older boys turn into the barnyard. "Someday," he vowed, "I will be the first one home!"

They slid from their sweaty mounts, pulled off the saddles and bridles, and began to brush them with currycombs. When they had turned them out to pasture, all three horses found grassy patches to roll in. The boys wandered up the hill to the house where they knew supper would soon be ready. Michael hoped they would have bread and milk soup tonight.

Michael knew that most people considered bread and milk soup to be poor man's food, but he didn't care. You simply broke slices of bread into chunks in a bowl, add milk and as much sugar as you could without getting caught. It was especially tasty if there were fresh strawberries or raspberries from the garden to add to the mix!

Sure enough, there was only bread and milk on the table when they sat down. After the blessing was prayed over the food, they all began to enthusiastically break the slices of bread into their bowls. Michael noticed the huge mixing bowl Carl was using for his soup bowl. Beside his bowl was a half loaf of bread designated for him only. Michael was impressed! "Wow," he said. "Daddy must be hungry!" An icy silence instantly fell over the table. Carl looked up from his bowl, and his cold gray eyes bored into Michael's chocolate brown eyes. It was a look that never failed to freeze the small boys in cold fear! It was like looking into the flat cold stare of a king cobra. "It just so happens"—Carl grated in a voice like the sound of the sleigh runners dragging across a naked rock in the woods—"that I do most of the work around here, and I *need* more to eat!" Michael couldn't even speak, much less apologize. He could only stare down at his plate and hope his father could for once control his insane fury, and he would not get a beating for what he had thought was an innocent remark. They all breathed easier when Carl began to eat again without further comment. Michael felt like he had escaped by a hair's breadth another beating as his father worked off his anger with his flailing leather belt. He thought that this must be how the field mice feel when the barnyard cats would catch them and play with them, batting them around with their paws as they tried desperately to escape the lightening-fast paws that would rake them back in toward the cat's head until the cat tired of the sport and crushed their tiny bodies. The feeling of utter helplessness only added to the paralyzing fear that greatly enhanced the physical pain of the beating. At their young ages, though, the boys could not understand that. They just tried hard to always avoid angering their father.

After supper, the boys headed back down the barn hill for the evening milking. Too small to be of much help, Michael was responsible for small things like cleaning up the cow poop in the walkways and sweeping those parts of the floor that could be swept. Their few cows gave pitifully little milk, and the chores were soon done. There was about a half hour of playtime left, then it would be time for bed. Although they hated bedtime, Charlotte managed to take some of the sting out of it by reading them bedtime stories. Never in his life would Michael remember his father tucking him in, reading, or praying with him; but his mother was quite faithful at reading to them. Public prayers offered in the Raptor house tended to be stuffy, emotionless, and formal rituals and, Michael was quite sure, a waste of time!

Tonight, Charlotte was finishing reading a book called *Welfare Kid*. It was a true but awful story about a cruel farmer who had taken in a young boy from the county welfare department solely for free help on the farm. The man was terribly abusive and wore a wide leather belt with which for little or no reason he would beat the poor scrawny welfare boy. Michael would shiver as the book described in horrific detail the welts and bruises constantly marking the boy's thin body from the cruel weapon. He stole a quick glance at his father, wondering if he might be taking a lesson from the evil man's cruelty. How could anyone be so mean to a little boy?

"Did you see how glued daddy was to the story when that mean guy was whipping that little boy?" Carl Jr. quietly asked Randy after the boys had crawled into bed and turned out the lights. They needed to be very quiet after lights out to avoid punishment, but sometimes, they would whisper in the dark.

"You just watch. He is going to get himself one of those wide belts too so he can whip us like that mean man did that little boy!" Carl Jr. declared.

Randy wasn't so sure. He often chose optimism over realism, a characteristic Michael often came to envy in him, but could never seem to emulate.

"You just wait and see," Carl Jr. repeated. The dark room was silent as they drifted off to sleep.

The next day, Carl announced his intention to go to town for some things he needed. He would take Carl Jr. along. Going along to town was always a coveted privilege, but they almost always had to take turns.

The day passed slowly with Randy and Michael helping their mother with housework and laundry and of course some weeding in the despised garden! *Why does anyone have a garden?* he wondered in disgust. Those nasty weeds are just horrid.

It was almost supper time when the old Chevy made its way up the lane. Randy and Michael raced out to meet it as it came to a stop in a cloud of dust. Sometimes, Carl would bring some candy or a small toy along home from town. Michael's brown eyes sparkled with excited hope as his father's door opened, and Carl climbed out. Then, the smile froze on his face and the sparkle in his eyes turned to stark disbelief! There was no candy or toy tonight. His eyes stared in horror at his father's waist. His scuffed old belt had been replaced. The new belt was wide and made of heavy leather, exactly like the belt the cruel man wore to beat the welfare kid!

*****

The summer days were getting hotter. Life could get boring for three little boys if none of them got creative. One of Michael's favorite activities was going exploring in the woods, but only if one of the older boys and Laddie went along for security purposes. The woods behind the house were his favorite. It was part of the main horse pasture, and he liked to walk the trails the horses made between their stomping areas. Rather than wander aimlessly through the woods, the horses tended to stick to trails they had made much like deer and other wildlife make. The impressive thing about the horses was that they would find cool, shady areas under large trees to stand and cool off, while they swished flies with their tails. In these areas, the grass and undergrowth would be wiped out by their stomping hooves as they tried in vain to fend off the persistent biting insects. One day, the boys explored even beyond the horse trails. Michael noticed that the trees were becoming more sparse and the underbrush thicker; then suddenly, they emerged on the shore of a small lake. It had no sandy sloping beach, and the brushy bank around it dropped directly into the water. They dropped to their stomachs on the bank and stared into the water. It was teeming with all kinds of fish.

"We gotta bring our fishing poles back here," Carl Jr. remarked excitedly.

"Yeah," Randy agreed, catching Carl Jr.'s enthusiasm. "I'll bet these would be easy to catch. Probably nobody even knows this lake is here!"

They were washing up for dinner in the old water basin in the porch after having shared with their mother all about their find and the vast quantities of enormous fish they would soon be catching. Randy reached up to dry his hands on the towel hanging on a nail, and his tattered shirt slid up exposing his flat stomach.

"I see the moon shining," Michael said, pointing at his belly button.

Grandma Raptor had once told him that, and he thought it was very funny. His grin froze on his face as he felt a powerful vise clamp around his left shoulder. He was jerked nearly off his feet as Carl dragged him outside and around the corner. He felt the familiar sick fear in his stomach he always got before a beating, but had no idea why he was getting one.

"Take your pants down!" Carl grated as he dragged the new belt from his waist. Trembling with fear and dread, Michael slid his short pants down to his ankles, praying he would not be forced to drop his shorts as well. It didn't hurt much more on bare skin than through his shorts, but the shame and humiliation of being beaten while exposed made the experience totally degrading.

"Your shorts too!" Carl commanded angrily.

Michael was shamefully sliding them down when the first blow from the heavy belt landed. The shock nearly tore the breath from his small body. He screamed and instinctively twisted to avoid the slashing belt, causing the next blow to cut across the soft flesh of his legs. His infuriated father grabbed him and held him between his knees, while he worked off his anger with the leather belt. Michael lost any sense of time, and eventually, he could no longer feel the searing pain of the belt biting his skin, only a deep jarring from the impact of the blows. Shock had deferred the pain to protect his consciousness. Everything was a hazy blur around him. He heard someone screaming and somewhere in his fuzzy brain realized it was him. Then, he felt the powerful knees release him, and he dropped to the ground where he lay gasping, choking on his sobs. He still had no idea what he had done wrong, but now, the penalty had been paid!

DEVIL IN THE BALER

Fall was in the air. The days were getting shorter and colder. School would soon be starting again, but first, the rest of the hay crop must be gathered into the haymows. Michael always liked the days they took the hay to Grandpa Raptor's barn. His haymow had the neatest mechanical system for unloading the wagon loads of loose grass hay. He had heard stories of wonder machines that would compress the hay into rectangular cubes and tie string around them to hold them in shape, but he had never actually seen one and was not sure he believed that they actually existed. How could any machine, no matter how ingenious, tie a knot in string?

He knew it was a big controversy among older folks too. He grinned as he thought back to the animated conversation he'd heard at a church carry-in dinner. Some of the older men were declaring rather emphatically that there is no way possible for those knotting rolls to make a knot when the knotting forks passed the twine through them.

"I'll tell you what's going on," one of the black clad brethren declared. "They put a hex on them machines at the factory, and they invite the devil in there to tie those knots!"

There was a moment of reflective silence; then, it was broken by farmer Nelson who was visiting from Ohio. He was an elderly man who was known for his progressive farming methods and no-nonsense approach to life in general.

"Let me tell you fellas something," he said calmly. "I heard that stuff, but I bought a baler anyway. And I learned something from firsthand experience. When those forks come up and pass through the knotting rolls and they *don't* make a knot, *that's* when the devil is in that baler!" Michael noted that the conversation had immediately taken a new direction.

For the Raptors, however, balers may as well not have existed. They made hay by hitching a team of horses to an ancient sickle-bar mower and circling the field, leaving fresh-smelling swaths of newly mown hay behind. A day or two later, it would be raked into long windrows; then, a team of horses pulling a hay wagon with a hay loader rumbling behind would circle the field, straddling the rows of dried hay. The hay loader was a tall and unwieldy beast, which, when hitched directly behind the hay wagon, towered over it. It was not quite as wide as the wagon and had in its day been a masterpiece of agricultural engineering. It was basically a tall, forward-sloping metal trough on big iron wheels with long forks moving in sequence to pick up the hay, move it up the trough, and dump it onto the wagon bed. There was always a man or two on the wagon to stack the hay on the wagon bed, creating a huge fluffy load of hay. The job of stacking hay on the wagon was not a coveted one for two reasons. First, the constant stream of hay dumped overhead created a constant cloud of hay dust. On a hot summer day, the sweat flowed freely, causing the dust and leaves from the hay to plaster on any exposed skin.

The second reason was the instability of the hay loader. Any serious jerk or lurch could upset it and cause it to come crashing forward and down on the back of the hay wagon. The hay stacker was often unable to move fast enough to avoid it completely because he would be standing knee-deep in fluffy loose hay, and many a man carried scars from accidents caused by upset hay loaders.

Today, Uncle Rusty was stacking the hay, and Carl Jr. was driving the loads to Grandpa Raptor's for unloading and then driving the empty wagons back to the hayfield. He was quite proficient at handling the team of sorrel draft horses, and Michael was romping atop the huge loads as the horses clip-clopped down the dusty gravel road. He became a bit uneasy as he noticed how close Carl Jr. was driving to the ditch. He never understood why his big brother got such a kick out of living on the edge. It seemed that whatever he did, if there was a way to make it more risky, then that is how he would do it. When he worked the fields with the ancient John Deere tractor, he would always go up the steepest part of the hill.

This would be the final load of the day. Michael soon tired of bouncing around atop the load and made himself a little nest where he laid on his back and let the warm sun lull him to sleep. He dreamed that he was on a playground, and the merry-go-round was swinging so hard he couldn't hang on any more. Now, he was shooting down the big slide at an alarming rate of speed! His little hands flailed wildly, trying to grasp the sides of the slide to slow his descent, but instead of the slide walls, he came up holding hay! The wagon was rolling over into the ditch, and the huge load of hay was sliding off with a very frightened Michael struggling to avoid being buried in the hay slide, and Carl Jr. trying desperately to control the frightened horses even as he rode the slide of hay into the waiting ditch.

Hours later, a group of very tired men and boys forked the last forkful of hay onto another wagon parked as close as they could get to the overturned wagon. Now, it was time to set the ditched wagon back on its wheels and pull it back up on the road. The team that had been pulling it had been tethered to a nearby tree. When the load of hay had been driven away, Carl untied the team and backed them to the side of the overturned wagon. He hitched a log chain high on the undercarriage of the wagon and clucked to the team. As the big draft horses leaned into their collars, the hardwood doubletree that made the connection from the harness to the chain began to rise as the chain tightened. Then, the wagon began to right itself, slowly at first and then faster and faster until it slammed back on its wheels, bouncing slightly from the impact. The damage was minimal, and Carl was able to hitch the team and head back to grandpa's farm.

They arrived at grandpa's barn just as the large iron forks were descending from the barn roof peak. This was Michael's favorite part. The barn roof had a peak extending out over the east end about ten feet. An iron track was fastened to the rafters, beginning at the peak and running the length of the roof. There was a large hinged door into the haymow that opened to allow access from the peak to the haymow. A rather complicated set of large forks on a trolley was operated by a huge hemp rope that ran through a series of pulleys and was hitched to a team of horses at the side of the barn. The forks were lowered to the wagon, and Carl planted them deeply into the loose hay on the wagon. Then at his signal, Grandpa clucked to his team who began to pull the rope. The forks began to rise toward the track, carrying a huge load of loose hay with them. When they reached the track, the rollers began to move the load into the haymow. In his hands, Carl held a much smaller rope tied to a trip mechanism on the mechanical forks. When the trolley reached the spot where he wanted the hay, Carl gave a mighty yank on the rope, releasing the catch and allowing the forks to swing open on their hinges. The resulting shower of yellow/green hay cascading to the haymow floor was a sight that never failed to impress the Raptor boys.

An hour later, the sweaty horses had been unharnessed and brushed down and were contentedly munching hay in their big wooden stalls. The Raptor crew made their way up the hill to grandma's house where a huge supper was already steaming on the table. The cows at home would get milked late tonight, but it was a good feeling to know that the hay loft was being filled with hay for the long hard winter ahead.

STORY BOXES AND SNEAKERS

Michael skipped down the rutted gravel road. It was getting easier all the time to keep up with his two older brothers on their way to Keefer's store. There was no way he could keep pace if they really hustled, but usually, the older boys wandered from ditch to ditch as they walked, looking for anything interesting. There was always an abundance of beer bottles thrown from the windows of the constantly inebriated Indians' rolling wrecks they called cars. Carl Jr., though, was looking for something useful, specifically partially smoked cigarette butts. He had taken to secretly carrying matches in his pockets, useful not only for starting fires in the woods and pastures but also for lighting cigarette butts he found.

"Hey, Randy!" he yelled triumphantly. "Look at this one!"

Randy looked with distaste at the half-smoked cigarette between Carl Jr.'s fingers. "That's gross!" he remarked. "Some drunk was slobbering on that butt, and now you're gonna put it in your mouth!"

Carl Jr. was too excited to stop and consider the invisible nasties that were probably crawling all over the butt. He lit a match and with some difficulty got the half-damp butt relit.

Smoking was only one bad practice the boys were picking up from their adopted uncle, Rusty. Carl Jr. was especially influenced by Uncle Rusty, who was into lying, stealing, smoking, drinking, and sexually molesting his young nephews. By now, Carl Jr. was starting to develop a real taste for the tobacco smoke. He had convinced Randy to try several times, but he had trouble getting past putting the filthy, second-hand butts in his mouth, so Carl Jr. just mostly enjoyed them by himself.

Hank's vicious mongrels greeted them with their usual rabid nastiness, punctuated by barking growls and snarls that froze Michael's legs in terror. He always glued himself to Carl Jr. or an adult when entering the store in the hope that he could make his escape while the monsters were ripping off the leg of his human shield!

They were barely inside the store today when they heard an unusual noise emanating from a large box sitting high on a shelf behind the sales counter. The box had a curved glass front, and Michael stared in fascination at the contraption. It just couldn't be! There were pictures moving around on the glass front of the box. He had never even heard of a television, and now, he was seeing one close up. A war movie was playing about a U.S. warship being stalked by a German submarine. The picture was black and white and rather indistinct, but to the three boys from the sticks, it was a veritable miracle. They were immediately drawn into the story and settled in to watch as the captain of the warship tried to determine if the little object floating several hundred yards off the port side was a piece of driftwood or the periscope of a German U-boat. The tension aboard the submarine was at fever pitch, and the crew had just loaded the torpedoes into their firing tubes and were about to launch when the ancient telephone behind the counter jangled noisily. Hank limped over and picked it up with a loud, "Hello." It was Charlotte instructing him to send the boys home. They groaned at the news and finally managed to tear themselves away from the marvelous box with its fascinating story.

They were still discussing it when they arrived back in the farmhouse and excitedly told Charlotte about the incredible storytelling box.

"Well," she remarked. "If I'd have known, then you could have stayed and finished the story."

After dinner, Carl ordered the boys to the barn to help harness horses for fieldwork. There always seemed to be an abundance of workhorses available, and he would hitch single horses to a section of harrow and have one of the small boys ride it for guidance. There was an art to riding a harnessed horse that included more dynamics than simply steering the big animal. When a small boy in short pants sits atop an eight-hundred-pound horse wearing a harness, he needs to be constantly on guard not to get his bare legs pinched in the continually moving and flexing harness parts. Also at five years of age, Michael had to be creative to climb on and off the huge animal. At the barn, he could lead the horse to the corral fence and climb up the fence and slip across to the horse's back. But out in the field, he had to climb up the harness one strap at a time like a small monkey climbing a tree.

After several hours of harrowing alone in the huge field, Michael was getting hot and bored. He wished he would have left his sneakers at home; his feet were so very hot. Suddenly, an idea struck him. He would climb down and take them off. The horse was only too happy to stop and let him clamber down. He pulled off the offending shoes and then wondered what to do with them. He looked at the furrowed ground he was harrowing and decided to just stick them into one of the furrows and harrow over them. For good measure, he scraped some loose dirt over them with his hands before climbing up and resuming his perch atop the horse. He watched with naive interest as the harrow passed over the spot, smoothing the loose dirt and leaving no trace of the grave site.

"Son, where are your shoes?" Carl asked on the way home that evening.

"They got hot so I buried them," Michael replied clueless as to the horrific offense he had committed.

"You did *what*?!" Carl roared.

"Well, my feet got hot, so I took them off and didn't know what to do with them," Michael replied. "You should have seen..." He looked at his father and froze with shock and terror! He knew that look from hard experience—the frozen features, the gray eyes, hard as slate with the ice-cold fire burning in them! He knew he was in for a beating, but even now, he didn't know exactly why. At five years of age, he simply didn't understand the sin of wasting scarce money by ruining even an old pair of sneakers.

The rest of the trip home passed in dead silence. He could sense that the fury was rising in his father by the minute! His fear was mounting accordingly, and by the time his father ordered him out behind the barn, his legs were trembling so badly he could hardly walk straight. Carl emerged from inside, and Michael's insides turned to ice as he saw the milking hose twitching in his powerful hand.

"Take your pants down!" Carl snarled. "I'll teach you to throw away good shoes!"

The humiliation of standing naked from the waist down didn't even register this time. He had never been beaten with a hose before, but once, he knew how badly it hurt from a time when Carl Jr. had accidentally hit his leg while swinging one. The heavy rubber hose hissed through the air like a venomous snake, biting the soft skin of his buttocks. Michael screamed from the searing pain, which seemed to encourage Carl's brutality. The hose became a constant blur of motion, slashing the buttocks and legs indiscriminately. Michael staggered and then was knocked to his knees by the force of the blows, his agonized screams echoed back from the empty forest beyond. There was no one to hear his agony, no one to rescue him from the fury-crazed man with the rubber hose! He stumbled to the ground beneath the blows and lay in a crumpled heap, no longer able to stand.

Finally, Carl had worked off his fury to a manageable level. Michael barely knew when he disappeared back into the barn to return the hose. His screams had turned to great racking sobs. He cried because he was such a horrible stupid child that his father had to beat him like an animal. He sobbed from the hurt of the fury and hate he had seen gleaming in the eyes of the father he loved. He wept because he had no hope of ever being a good boy!

*****

A few weeks later, Charlotte was in a cleaning frenzy. "Grandpa Reynolds are coming from Ohio and bringing some teachers for summer Bible School, so I want you to clean up and be ready right after dinner," she told the boys.

"I hope Aunt Olivia comes again," Randy remarked. "She's the nicest aunt we've got."

They were just finishing washing the dishes and cleaning up the kitchen when a car horn sounded coming up the driveway.

"They're here!" shouted Carl Jr. racing for the door.

Grandpa's long, sleek Chrysler came to a stop in a swirl of dust. Although the family business acumen had never seemed to quite reach to grandpa, by the Raptors' economic standards, he was rich. His cars were late models, while Carl always observed a three-hundred-dollar spending limit on any vehicle he purchased to replace the totally fatigued family car.

To their great delight, Aunt Olivia was in the car, along with her seventeen-year-old daughter Jeanie. As the car doors opened and people began climbing out, Michael spied a figure that stopped him in his tracks. *Oh no!* he thought. *She came too!* "She" was Aunt Bridget, the oldest sister of the Reynolds clan, and the Raptor boys saw her as the "battle axe" of the bunch. She said whatever came to her mind and wasted no words on politeness or niceties to spare others' feelings. Michael was just plain scared of her and tried to stay out of her way as much as possible.

When the "Hellos" and "My how you've growns" were finally out of the way, Grandpa walked around behind the car and opened the lid of its massive trunk. It was packed full of used clothes for the Raptors and food for the coming week. Charlotte flushed slightly when she saw the food. It was a point of pride with her and Carl to make their own way without charity, and no matter how scarce the money was, between the huge garden and the beef and pork in the barnyard, their family would never know hunger.

Grandma seemed to sense her embarrassment and said, "When we bring a big group like this for a week, the least we can do is bring a little food along to help out!" That seemed to help restore Charlotte's wounded dignity, and the supplies were carried in and stacked in the dining room.

COUSIN HENRY

Supper was ready by the time the guests had been shown to their rooms and bathed off the grime from the many miles of travel over dusty gravel roads with all the car windows open. Grandpa's cars were nice, but still a long way from the future marvel of air conditioning. With no indoor plumbing, bathing was done in a large galvanized metal tub with water carried in and heated on the kitchen stove. A small room was created just off the porch with blankets strung up on ropes to ensure privacy.

The old farmhouse was not large, with a conjoined kitchen and dining room, living room, and master bedroom on the lower floor and two bedrooms upstairs. Carl had hung blankets in the basement to make extra rooms down there for the boys and some of the cousins. Michael found the change exciting, but Carl Jr. noticed that the cousins who shared their accommodations found it less impressive, especially Aunt Olivia's outspoken son Henry. He was about six years older than Carl Jr. and feared neither man nor beast. Even Carl Jr. was often impressed by his daring stunts, not to mention his sassy wisecracks to adults who he considered a bit too impressed with themselves. Almost everyone agreed though, Henry was a very funny guy!

After supper, the aunts began to open the large cardboard boxes of used clothes. Michael kept a wary eye on Aunt Bridget as he tried to hang close to Aunt Olivia. She had him try on a long parade of shirts, trousers, and shoes. He was beginning to think that maybe he would completely escape Aunt Bridget's acid tongue when he heard her call his name. He slowly turned toward her and saw that she was holding a shirt and eyeing him speculatively, so he sidled over and was about to stick his arm into one of the sleeves when he heard her rasp, "Stop right there, young man! You go change that filthy T-shirt before you even think of trying on these clean clothes!" He obligingly scampered out of her grasp and tried to spend enough time changing the offending T-shirt so she would forget about him trying on the shirt. By the time he returned, the fittings were nearly through, and to his relief, Cousin Jeanie helped him try it on again. He made a mental note to walk softly around Aunt Bridget this week and avoid her at all costs. He had heard that her husband had fallen over and died at a very young age from a heart attack and wondered if that was what made her so mean. Actually, he really couldn't blame her husband. If he would be married to a woman like that, he decided a heart attack would be a good way to get some relief!

Later as everyone was beginning to settle in for the night, Carl Jr. nudged Michael and said quietly, "Let's go to the toilet. I want to show you something!" They headed for the outdoor structure behind the garage, but as they passed grandpa's car, Carl Jr. glanced around furtively and then dodged behind the car and opened the trunk with the key that had been conveniently left in the lock. He opened it, and the huge cavity appeared totally empty. "Look here," Carl Jr. whispered as he reached into a barely noticeable crevasse under the backseat. He pulled out a medium-sized box of chewing tobacco. Grandpa had chewed tobacco all his life and carried a supply with him.

The box was covered with the bright, gaudy logo of the tobacco company and had a lid mounted on two tiny brass hinges. Carl lifted the lid to reveal two rows of rolled-up tobacco neatly packaged in waxed paper. He carefully removed one roll and slipped it into the pocket of his tattered jeans.

He then carefully replaced the box and closed the trunk with a soft click. The entire episode had taken less than a minute, and they continued on to the outhouse where Carl Jr. stashed his loot under the floorboards. "Don't you say a word to anyone about this!" he warned fiercely. "This is gonna give me fixins for a lot of smokes."

Several nights later, the boys had been sent to their basement bedrooms for the night. By now, Henry had become the official

65

comedian of the junior league. Tonight's entertainment began with him mimicking some of the goofy-sounding people he had encountered on this trip, with a few of the less liked adults thrown in for good measure. The Raptor boys tried to keep their laughter quiet, but when he graduated to making farting noises with his hand under his armpit, they burst out laughing. Charlotte called several warnings down the stairs for them to settle down, each sounding a bit more frustrated than the one before. Finally, she called down in an ominous tone, "Boys, am I gonna hafta send dad down?"

"*Sure!*" Henry called back up. "Send him on down!"

The Raptor boys were aghast!

"Henry, shut up!" Carl Jr. hissed. "You're gonna get us killed!"

"Naw," Henry replied. "He's not gonna do anything to you when I'm here to see it."

This logic was new to them, and they considered it for a while; then, decided it would be prudent not to put it to the test. One by one, they drifted off to sleep.

*****

With the added busyness of summer Bible school at the little church, the Raptor house was chaotic. Carl had never been able to handle stress well, and the boys learned to avoid him as much as possible. They would do their chores as quickly as possible to avoid being in his presence and lived in almost constant fear that some small act or oversight on their part would set off his volcanic temper, causing him to lash out with a blow from his hand or boot. Michael preferred the kicks to the blows because they normally landed on the lower body. Although they were equally painful, there was less psychological impact than seeing and feeling the powerful hand smash into his head or face. He often felt sorry for Carl Jr. who as the oldest child was forced to spend much more time assisting his father and was therefore directly in line for the abuse spewed out when his temper blew out and he needed release! Carl could overlook quite a bit of boyish incompetence when he was in a good mood, but the tiniest infraction would induce violent retribution when he was upset.

It helped now, though, that there was so much company around. It was necessary for Carl to haul the offending child far enough away from the visitors that they wouldn't hear the blows landing on flesh and screams of fear and pain.

"Everybody pile in," Grandpa said. "Time to go to Bible school!" His car was soon jammed full of excited kids. The adults would ride in the Raptor's car. Today, Grandpa would cruise the gravel roads picking up community kids. Michael got irritated and sometimes embarrassed by the uncivilized antics of the half-breed community kids. They would say the stupidest stuff, which the visiting teachers found uproariously funny. One of the aunts, for example, loved to tell about how she had finally gotten her young charges settled enough to ask, "Who has a song you'd like to sing?" A young Indian girl with a serious face and huge black eyes popped her hand up and said, "Pistol Packin' Momma!"

Michael was too young to understand the horrible social and unsanitary living conditions that formed these children's lives. Alcohol abuse was rampant across the reservation, and at very young ages, Indian and half-bred children regularly witnessed adults fighting, beating each other unconscious, knife fights, rapes, and every form of violence known to man. Some of them had even witnessed murders, although they would never speak of it to the authorities when they came around doing their halfhearted investigations.

The yard of the little gray stucco church was filled with excited children, playing and shouting, ready to start Bible school week. It was one of the highlights of the community and something the little church did well. There were the usual stars and stickers for attendance and verses learned, lessons completed, etc. Michael loved it all with two exceptions. He had an incredible memory for reciting Bible passages, and while other children could stand and read their memory verses from "cheat sheets," Charlotte was adamant that his be done from memory. He was given entire chapters to memorize, and when he focused, he could learn them easily, but who wanted to focus on long boring Bible passages when there was ball to play and tepees to build out in the surrounding woods? Somehow, he managed to get them all learned by program night, and more than once, visiting adults would single him out after the program and embarrass him with praise and encouragement for his impressive recitations.

The other thing he disliked was the special music part. He had a natural musical ear and the ability to sing any of the three parts his adolescent voice could manage. It came so naturally to him that he could even switch parts in every word of the slower songs. As a result, he and Randy were in constant demand for special music performances. He loved to sing, but he would never enjoy the public scrutiny of standing before live audiences to perform for them. In his heart, he just knew they were all laughing at him. If someone blew their nose, he was sure they were hiding a smile in their handkerchiefs; if a fly landed on their face making them twitch, he had no doubt that the resulting facial twitch was an out-of-control smirk. And if, God forbid, anyone yawned, there was no doubt in his mind that he and Randy were boring the bat snot out of them!

Finally, the front door opened, and Pastor Oliver stepped out and rang the large brass bell. With a shout, the children from all over the yard rushed to assemble at the base of the large concrete stairs leading up to the big double doors of the church. Summer Bible school was officially in progress. The teachers moved through the unruly little mob, sorting out classes by age and grades and gently shushing little "potty mouths." The local church children rolled their eyes and snickered at the crude and inappropriate remarks but were careful not to let the grownups see them laugh. Their parents had let them know that they were supposed to be an example to the community kids.

When the little crowd was finally sorted out, they filed noisily into the little chapel. The pews were handmade from pine boards that had been harvested and sawed from trees that had been cut to clear the area for the chapel. They were plain but sturdy and had been repeatedly scarred by bored children and varnished so many times they became sticky on very hot and humid days. Carl Jr. and his friend, Pastor Oliver's oldest son Danny, had their own little program going during the opening songs and comments and were so deeply engrossed in their private exchange that they failed to hear the superintendent ask the group to stand for prayer. This was rather unusual because in this church they nearly always knelt for group prayer. The boys snapped to attention as the kids around them began moving and realized that they too should be in motion. Without looking around, they twisted rapidly and slid to their knees. Too late, they realized that they had blown it and were now the focus of everyone around them. Randy giggled out loud; Bible school was getting fun already!

CORDUROYS

The first rays of the morning sun were touching the curtains in the boys' bedroom as Michael began to stir. His foggy consciousness was beginning to assimilate the confusing sound of someone singing. *Oh no!* he thought groggily. *It's mom's wakeup song!* Charlotte and Carl each had their own distinctive ways of waking the boys. When Carl woke them, it was usually still dark and time to head for the barn to begin the morning chores. He would clomp up the varnished hardwood stairs and into the room. As he reached for the light switch, he would say, "Boys, watch your eyes," and then flip the lights on. Michael always dreaded those four words, especially in the winter when he would have to crawl out from under the warm mountain of blankets onto the ice-cold hardwood floors. By the time they managed to get into their freezing cold clothes, they would often be shivering too hard to get the buttons closed properly. Often, they would grab their clothes and race downstairs to stand on the huge register where the first warmth from the huge furnace in the basement was beginning to rise to the main floor.

Charlotte, however, had a different wakeup style. While Michael would often be up before her during the long days of summer, he would usually still be in bed like his brothers when the days became shorter and colder. Charlotte would breeze into the room singing, "Good morning to the flowers. Good morning to the sun. Good morning to the boys and girls. Good morning everyone."

"School today," she announced cheerily. Michael groaned silently. *School*, he thought disgustedly, *what a waste of time!* He wished for the hundredth time that his friend "Dode" would go to his school. He and Dode would often spend Sunday afternoons

70

together, and sometimes, they would ride their horses the nine miles between their farms to be together.

First, however, came the never-ending barn chores. Michael's thoughts brightened as he remembered the new twin Holstein calves in the barn. Because of his small size, he had been put in charge of feeding the calves.

He was soon trudging down the hill to the ramshackle barn in his oversized hand-me-down boots. He heard the grinding hum of the ancient cream separator as he rounded the corner and stepped over the rotting threshold into the dingy room that housed the separating machine. The separator machine always fascinated him, and he stopped for a moment and watched as Carl Jr. entered with two galvanized buckets of fresh warm milk and dumped them into the pot-bellied stainless steel hopper atop the contraption. Randy then began to turn the iron crank on the side; and in a few moments, thick rich cream began to flow out of a short spout protruding from one side of the machine and thin, watery skim milk from another spout and into the calf feeding bucket. When two buckets were approximately half full, Michael picked them up and headed for the calf pen. Randy was always careful to put equal amounts of milk in each bucket, but when Michael was out of his sight, he would surreptitiously dump a small amount from one into the other. Although he really didn't know why, he preferred the baby heifer over her little bull brother and would always give her more of the warm, watery milk.

He sometimes felt guilty about this unfair treatment and even wondered why he preferred the heifer. He assuaged his conscience at times by telling the baby calves, "Okay, first come first serve!" But when the little bull would get there first, he would sometimes change it to, "First come, worst serve."

Several years later, he overheard his parents discussing how those twin calves were born the same size and the little heifer grew so much faster than the bull. Young as he was, he hadn't even noticed the difference in growth; he was just taking care of his little heifer!

When the chores were finished and breakfast was over, the boys made half-hearted efforts at washing up for school and then headed upstairs to change into school clothes. Bathing in a cold house with no running water was a once-a-week affair, and it never occurred to them that they just might not be totally clean under those school clothes. As for smell, the kids at the one room school all smelled the same since none of them had running water either!

Today though, there was one big highlight for Michael, a pair of brand new shoes! Usually, it was Carl Jr. who got all the new clothes and shoes. As the oldest child, he would soon outgrow them, and they would be passed down the line to smaller brothers until the last shred of use had been squeezed out of them. But the last pair of school shoes hadn't made it past Randy, so Michael had hit the footwear jackpot!

Carl and Charlotte did their best to keep their children looking somewhat respectable and for the most part did quite well given the extreme shortage of cash, except for the corduroys! Charlotte loved the toughness of the rough fabric, and they were relatively inexpensive. They would be one of the things from his childhood Michael would hate forever. In later years, when they were bussed to the big schools in town, they were a constant source of embarrassment to him. He could handle the cool farmer's boots the other white kids wore in contrast to his scuffed, hand-me-down sneakers, but the ultracool denim Levi's were a thing to covet! The Levi's only got cooler as they faded, while the corduroys got faded, threadbare, and even more ugly (if that were possible) and lasted forever! Sartorial splendor was just not an option for dirt-poor missionary kids!

The air was still chilly as the boys began the half-mile hike to the little one-room county schoolhouse. While there was little safety risk, the walk always kinda spooked them. Since the fear of monsters hadn't been invented yet, the Raptor boys had only three main fears—bears, drunk Indians, and kidnappers, in that order! Mounted on their horses, they had no fears of any of these and rode anywhere any time, even in deep twilight. But the little county school was not equipped to board horses during the school day, so they had to walk. And on foot, these courageous young equestrians were, well, chickens!

The crisis, when it came, didn't happen on a school day but on a Saturday morning. Carl Jr. and Randy were walking along the road when they heard the sound of a car approaching in the distance. True to form, they beat a hasty retreat into the tall grass of the field beside the road. They lay flat on their stomachs and tried not to move at all. To their horror, the car slowed as it got closer and then stopped altogether where the boys had left the road for the field. All was silent for a time; then, Carl Jr. summoned the courage to slowly raise his head and cautiously peek through the weeds toward the car.

"There are two men in the car," he whispered. "And they are looking this way!" Randy didn't respond; he was too busy attempting to literally become one with mother earth. "Oh no!" Carl Jr. hissed. "They're loading a rifle!"

By now, he had guessed that the men had mistaken the movement in the grass for a deer, so he did the only thing he could think to do. He popped up like a jack-in-the-box and waved his arms as he yelled, "Hi there!" The men looked startled, then replaced the rifle, and sped away. Two shaken boys hastily made their way back to the farm.

*****

One afternoon in late fall, Carl took Carl Jr. with him to pick up some supplies about twenty-five miles from home. It wasn't a terribly long drive even on the rutted gravel roads and with the dilapidated and increasingly undependable old Ford. However, the road passed through a huge forest known to be the home of some of the most dangerous wild beasts around.

Their business took much longer than Carl had anticipated, and it was nearly dark by the time they set off for home. They were about a third of the way into the huge forest when the old car began a death dance, coughing and sputtering. Carl coaxed a few more miles out of it before it gave one last mighty pop and died. No amount of coaxing and tinkering could bring it back to life. They had no flashlight, and it was a dark and moonless night, making visibility extremely poor. They began to walk to the closest house, which was approximately a seven-mile distance at the edge of the big forest. Carl Jr. was finding it a bit creepy and walked as close to his father as he could. He didn't get real scared until his father stopped stock still and silent. Then, Carl Jr. heard a sound that sent an icy finger of fear all the way up his spine.

Something was in the bushes directly beside them, only a few feet away, and it was stalking them! Carl located the largest stick he could find in the darkness and began to smack it on bushes, rocks, and anything that would create noise as he shouted and talked loudly, hoping to intimidate the beast. When they moved, the stalker moved, and when they stopped, it stopped. By now, Carl Jr. realized that his father was nearly as scared as he was, and that terrified him even more. He had never seen his father afraid of anything or any-one, and if he was scared, they were in real trouble! The stalker kept pace with them all the way through the forest, but they got not one glimpse of it. Carl later said he thought it was a wildcat, but for some reason, maybe because their impassioned prayers, it never attacked.

They reached the nearest house shortly after midnight, rousing the farmer from a sound sleep. He was kind enough to give them a ride home, where a thoroughly exhausted Carl Jr. collapsed into bed and slept the sleep of the dead! They would never know what had stalked them through the forest that long dark night, but there was no question that that forest was full of animals that were fully capable of tearing them to pieces.

THE WICKSONS

The boys arrived at the little white schoolhouse just as the teacher was walking out on the porch to ring the school bell. The noisy chaos of children's games began to subside as the students began to line up for the morning recitation of the Pledge of Allegiance. The teacher, Miss Hart, with the help of several community mothers arranged the rowdy bunch into approximate age groups on the lawn at the base of the wooden stairs leading up to the front porch of the school-house and then managed to get them quiet for the solemn recitation. Although most of the smaller children didn't really understand the flag and what all it stood for, it was a time in America when true patriots governed the nation. The flag was honored for all the thousands of men and women who had pledged their wealth and loyalty and even sacrificed their lives for the greatest nation the world had ever seen. The self-centered liberals who would later burn and desecrate her would never have been tolerated! The pledge was recited solemnly with heads bared and right hands pressed over hearts.

Then the new school year began, with children crowding and jostling each other to get into the school room. Miss Hart organized the students into classes with the younger classes up front and ages increasing as you progressed toward the back of the room. Michael found himself sitting across the aisle from Kenney Rawson. The Rawsons were an interesting white family who were one hundred percent "redneck" before the term was even invented! Nate, the father, was a tall broad-shouldered man with only a few yellow teeth and a booming voice that always carried an authoritative tone. He was also considered the community's foremost authority on anything horse related. His overgrown farm with its tumbledown buildings was located fifteen miles back a poorly maintained gravel road and deep in the forest, where he kept a large herd of horses.

Michael had been there several times with Carl and inwardly marveled at the deference Carl had shown Nate as he worked his mostly wild horse herd. It was a thrilling sight to see the wild, proud splendor of the horses milling excitedly around the crude corral made of sturdy Tamarack poles. Nate's rope loop would hiss across the corral over the heads of the herd and settle around the neck of the horse he had chosen. If the horse was not broken, the ensuing demonstration of horsemanship would be worthy of any performance before the cheering throngs at official rodeo events.

Kermit, however, was the physical opposite of his father, a small, slight and timid boy who was easily pushed around by his rowdier schoolmates. It was a dog-eat-dog world where there was no substitute for brawn and courage. The strong dominated the weak, and the males ruled the females.

Michael risked a quick look over his right shoulder toward the "school library" at the back of the room. It consisted of several shelves full of tattered, dog-eared books, which were unimpressive by anyone's standards. But to a small budding bookworm, they held the power to magically sweep one into worlds of indescribable adventure and excitement. There were two children's books that especially fascinated him his first two years in this school. His number one favorite was an illustrated book about a milkman and his horse-drawn wagon called *The Horse That Takes The Milk Around*. His close second was *Flip And The Cows*, a story about a timid young foal named Flip who conquered his deep fear of cows.

Michael who lived in almost constant fear could easily identify with the colt. But while Flip managed to overcome his fears by jumping the creek, a little missionary boy on an Indian reservation had to live with his, and nights especially were a thing to be feared!

He was rudely snapped back to attention by the nasal hiss of the girl seated directly behind him. Delilah Wickson would be a continual thorn in his flesh for as long as he attended this school. The Wicksons were a half-breed family who lived several miles past grandpa's farm and basically epitomized classlessness! They existed on welfare and charity and were totally unencumbered by cultural or social graces. The girls Delilah and Dorothy, her older and equally esthetically unpleasing older sister, were easily identifiable in any crowd as the girls with filthy hair, tattered and dirty clothes, and runny noses. Delilah had a permanent crush on Michael, while Dorothy tended to divide her affections between Randy and Carl Jr.

Dorothy had managed to totally alienate the easygoing Randy however one Sunday morning when the Raptors were taking her home from church. It was the beginning of a new Sunday school quarter, so the students had been issued new study books. Randy had written his full name on his, Randy Benjamin Raptor. Dorothy noticed his name and let out an irritating cackle of gravelly laughter. Then, she said, "Charlotte, Charlotte, Randy wrote bajamas on his church book!" Randy had to endure a lot of teasing about writing bajamas on his church book, but in time, the humor of it faded.

Michael, however, would be teased unmercifully for years about the stupid things Delilah would say in her bad, slobbery speech, mostly because she kept furnishing his tormentors with a stream of new material. Randy's personal favorite was her comment that "Michael's my boycee" (boyfriend) and "I kith em n kith em, n kith em!"

It was enough to gag a maggot, without the fact of Randy and Carl Jr. gleefully quoting it for years to anyone who showed the slightest interest.

The rheumy hiss came again, and Michael rasped back over his shoulder, "Shut up! We're in school!" Chastened, she slouched down in her desk to munch on what was left of her fingernails. *Oh yeah*, Michael thought. *It's gonna be a long year!* He reached for the textbook Miss Hart was handing him and thumbed through it with mild interest. Subjects like math and science bored him. Really, who cared about numbers, atoms, cells, or protoplasm? Literature and stories were what interested him and even history, where real people actually did interesting stuff, like kill each other off and take their horses and land. Now that was real life!

The day crawled by with two recess breaks and lunch break at noon. Miss Hart insisted that everyone play outside and enjoy the beautiful autumn weather, although Michael would have rather spent recess looking at the library books. The Raptor boys were active but not athletic, and there were really no good athletes in the school, so everyone was welcome to play softball, making the games only as fun as the performance of the poorest players. But it was a way for children to work off their surplus energy so they could concentrate better on their studies. Sometimes, the older boys were allowed to pump buckets of water from the ancient hand pump in front of the school and carry them over to Keefer's store. Mr. Keefer had no well and relied on the school pump for his water. He would usually give the boys a few cents for carrying him water when school was in session. The boys might even be fortunate enough to get a few minutes opportunity to watch his incredible picture box!

Later that night when the lights were turned out, Michael lay in bed considering life. There were so many bad and scary things in life, but some good things too and even some fun stuff. But really, there was only one thing that was always good—the horses. In a couple of years, he would have his own horse. Carl always gave each boy a horse of his own when he was nine or ten, and Michael would soon be old enough. Tonight, if he was lucky, he would dream about horses instead of the horrible huge, twisting black thing!

DUSTY

"Well kids," Carl said. "How about going to the sale barn this evening?"

"Sure," the boys chorused. "What are we gonna buy?"

"Well, I don't know if they will have what we want or not," he said. "But it's about time for Randy to have his own horse."

"Wow!" Randy said. "That would be great!"

With supper and the chores finished, they piled into the old Chevy and headed for the sale barn in Cedar Lake. Charlotte had decided to stay home and get caught up on a few things. She would enjoy the peace and quiet and maybe get to bed early.

Arriving at the sale barn, Carl parked the car in the gravel parking lot and led the three boys to the horse area of the sale barn. They took their time looking them over, but nothing really seemed to be what Randy needed. They found seats in the stands anyway and listened to the hypnotic chant of the auctioneer. Soon, the first horse came through, followed by a procession of others, of all colors, breeds, and sizes. Carl bid on a few but let them all pass; nothing seemed quite right for a good price. Finally, near the end of the sale, a dun-colored mare was brought through with a beautiful buckskin yearling colt at her heels.

"Sell them separately," the owner instructed. The mother was soon sold for more than Carl was planning to spend. Then, the auctioneer began trying to get a bid on the colt. Carl looked at Randy who was smitten with the little fellow. "Let's buy him dad," he said. "I'll wait for him to grow up and then train him myself!"

The auctioneer had finally gotten a bid of fifteen dollars and was trying for twenty when Carl joined the competition. Slowly, the bid crawled upward to thirty dollars; then, the other bidder raised to twenty-five. Carl was not sure by now that this was a good idea and asked Randy, "Are you sure he's what you want?" Randy nodded vigorously, and the auctioneer observing the gesture raised the bid to twenty-seven dollars. The other bidder had bid high enough, and after trying unsuccessfully to raise the bid, the auctioneer banged his gavel on the scarred wooden bench and said, "*Sold* to the young man up there behind Carl Raptor!"

The boys rushed down to the pens to see him close up, while Carl paid the bill and arranged for a truck to deliver him. The colt was beautiful, with his creamy buckskin coat and black mane and tail. But he was rather skittish, since no one had spent time with him, and he was rather scared. Michael thought about *Flip And The Cows* and felt sorry for him. When it came to understanding scared, he was an expert!

"I'm gonna name him Dusty," Randy said. "'Cuz he looks kinda dusty."

The boys could hardly contain their eager anticipation the next day until the truck arrived carrying the colt. He was unloaded and turned out to the pasture with the other horses and immediately became the focus of their interest. He tried to avoid them, but they just followed him around, crowding and snuffling at him. Finally, he had had enough. He tore across the pasture with the others hard on his heels. Carl was impressed. "That little guy is fast!" He said. That was music to Randy's ears. Carl Jr. was consistently winning their races with the filly he had trained, and he would love to beat him. Little could he know that none of them would ever see Dusty lose a race!

*****

Sunday dawned crisp and clear. It seemed to Michael that every Sunday was sunny and beautiful. He wondered seriously at times if that was why they were called Sunday as in the day the sun shines, but, after thinking it through, thought there was probably another reason for names of days of the week.

Pastor Oliver was absent this morning, and the old missionary pastor Randy was officiating in the service. Pastor Randy was the man who had started the little mission here, and though he was gone a lot on missionary trips and visiting, he with his wife and granddaughter kept a small mobile home on the Raptor farm, which he had built himself. It was a rather crude, metal-covered creation, and somewhere in his electric wiring, the grounding system had gone bad. When you touched the trailer with your bare hands, you wouldn't notice anything wrong if you were wearing shoes, which the grownups always did. But it was a very different story for little barefoot boys and especially so if it had rained and the ground was damp. The older boys had figured out how to open the metal door with a rag or glove, but Michael just avoided it altogether. He had another reason besides the electric shock—Sporty, the huge black Labrador. While his parents liked him around to help Laddie discourage the native marauders, he was getting grouchier and snappier with age, and Michael never forgot being dragged through the snow as a little child. A single stare from those malevolent eyes was enough to chill his blood, and a menacing growl would freeze him in his tracks!

Usually, Pastor Randy's sermons geared toward adults and delivered in an unenthused monotone were good times for little boys to zone out mentally and focus their thoughts on more interesting things, the substance of which varied with age. While Michael and Dode were thinking about horses, Carl Jr. would usually be thinking about Maria or one of her friends, and Uncle Rusty would be thinking about almost anyone wearing a skirt.

Today, however, Michael sat spellbound as Pastor Randy spoke. He wasn't always easy to understand; with his German accent, he interchanged his v's and w's. Usually, it was easy to figure out what he was trying to say; but one evening, he was telling the children a story for children's class; and in the story, some missionary kids had gotten trapped way up high on a cliff, and the only escape from the bloodthirsty savages who were stalking them was down the face of the cliff to the river a hundred feet below. They had no rope, so they twisted vines together and slid down on them. Only, he said *wines* instead of *vines*, and Michael had been lost for the rest of the story trying to visualize kids sliding down wine ropes; it just didn't make sense!

This morning, he was as agitated as Michael had ever seen him. The nation was having a presidential election, and for the first time ever, a Catholic man, a Mr. Kennedy, was running for president. Michael wasn't sure exactly what a Catholic was, but Pastor Randy was graphically explaining what they were. The Catholics, he emphasized, were gaining control of the nation one institution at a time. They already controlled the banks and financial institutions, the workplaces, businesses, law enforcement departments, the press, and the list went on and on. And now, he rumbled ominously, they were trying to take over the government at its highest level! If that happened, he warned, their way of life would be altered forever. "The Catholic church leaders," he said, "give us a child until he's six, and he will be a Catholic for life."

On the drive home, Michael wondered how soon the Catholics would come for them. His mind teemed with unanswered questions. What did they look like? Where did they hide out while they waited to grab people and destroy their lives? He stared deep into the passing forests. Was that odd dark shape perhaps a Catholic getting ready to pounce? It was all just so scary, but he didn't dare ask anyone about it because the other boys would make fun of him. He would just have to be careful, and store these fears with all the others in his life.

That evening, they had church again. Evening church was not as long as morning church, and the children's classes were usually more interesting than the morning Sunday school classes. Tonight would be a memorable one. It was presented by one Rosella Hofenvagan, a lady from the community who had joined the church. She had no husband but brought her two daughters, Joy, who was in Michael's opinion as attractive as an aging coonhound, and Carrie, who was the Raptor boys all agreed downright homely! Rosella herself was a large rawboned woman with a lumpy build and a face that bore a remarkable resemblance to a very old cow. Her voice was, however, her most memorable characteristic. It was, Michael thought, sort of a combination of the grating sound the dump rake made when it was overdue for a grease job and phlegmy wheeze Delilah Wickson made when she had a bad cold and ran around on the playground in the winter.

Tonight, though, would be extra special. Rosella had recently heard a new song and couldn't wait to sing it for them. Michael thought her weird voice actually made her stories a little more interesting, so maybe, the same would be true of her singing. It wasn't! The song started out unbelievably horrible and then went downhill from there. Her voice wheezed, wobbled, and croaked, and whatever the lyrics said was lost on the grinning and snickering children. Michael glanced furtively at the adults and noticed that they all looked unusually happy too for some reason. His father had his head down and was busily looking through his Bible with a barely controlled twitch at the corners of his mouth. Mrs. Hofenvagan ground her way through what seemed like all fifteen verses of the song and then closed on a long drawn-out wobbly note for dramatic effect. "Now, wasn't that a meaningful song?" she asked. No one in the audience could possibly have disagreed with her on that point, although their perspectives might have been rather different than hers!

FORTY BELOW ZERO

"We are gonna have to move," Carl announced one evening over supper. "The house is in bad need of repairs, so we are going to spend the winter in the back of the garage."

"The garage?" Carl Jr. said, looking puzzled. "There's no house back there!"

"Well, Pastor Randy and I are going to make a temporary apartment back there," Carl stated.

After the breakfast dishes were washed and put away, Randy and Michael hurried out behind the garage to see what was happening. Pastor Randy and their father were busily nailing up boards for a divider wall, making a room across the full width of the garage and approximately fifteen feet deep. It was necessary to keep it small because there would be no insulation, and the sole source of heat would be a small, tin, airtight stove. There was one entrance door from the side, which entered directly into a makeshift kitchen and dining area, at the far side of which sat the potbellied stove, nearly at the center of the room. On the wall behind the stove, they nailed boards horizontally across two wall studs, creating a crude ladder up to the ceiling, where they cut a trap door to the upper floor. The boys would need to sleep upstairs where the only heat would be from what filtered up through the cracks in the ceiling above the little stove. It seemed like a great adventure to them. There were only a couple small windows in the main floor and none at all upstairs. There was only room for the most essential furnishings.

A few days after they had moved in, the first blizzard struck with the howling ferocity of a wild beast! The small windows frosted over with a thick coat of ice, and drafts of ice-cold air knifed in through the many small cracks in the tarpaper-covered walls. Movement outside was nearly impossible, so the family was restricted to the tiny apartment. The boys couldn't hang out in their rooms unless they buried themselves in their beds under mountains of blankets, so they all squeezed into the tiny main floor apartment. They read books, played table games, ate, and napped. Carl was almost constantly feeding the little airtight stove, which was putting forth a heroic effort to keep the room tolerably warm. Michael noticed that if you stood close to the stove, his front would become uncomfortably warm, while at the same time, his back was uncomfortably cold. The outhouse was only about thirty feet from the front door, but using it in this weather was pure misery, so they visited it as little as possible.

Chores were exercises in freezing misery. The cattle and horses were crowded into the drafty little barn and were eating their way through the winter's supply of hay at an alarming rate. They did only the absolutely necessary things like milk the cows, fork hay into the mangers, and turn them out for a few minutes so they could drink water from the huge iron water tank. The horses fared best because they had grown warm, shaggy coats of hair, while the cows' hair was much shorter, and their udders and teats were vulnerable to the cold. When these ferocious winter blizzards set in, people and animals suffered through them in survival mode.

The third morning of the blizzard, Michael awoke early as usual. He surveyed the frigid room, locating all his clothes and shoes, then leaped out of bed, hastily collected them, and scampered down the ladder like a squirrel. Carl was standing beside the little stove, which he had just overfilled with dry wood. It was crackling and making a dull roaring sound as the blizzard winds sucked the smoke up the chimney. Carl looked concerned, and wordlessly, Michael followed his gaze to the sides of the tin stove, which were glowing red. If the sides melted down, the stove would collapse, almost certainly burning the entire garage down! Carl tried pouring a little water into the door of the stove, but the superhot fire turned it instantly to steam and spat it back at him. There was nothing to do but wait and pray that the little stove would hold up, which it did. Gradually, the sides turned from orange red to cherry red and then dark red until they were again black.

The day passed slowly, and by late afternoon, the howling wind began to die down. Michael blew on an ice-covered window until a small round spot melted off, allowing him to see out. The landscape was like pictures he had seen of Antarctica or the North Pole. The trees and bushes were coated with snow and ice and huge snowdrifts covered the ground all the way to the woods. Nothing moved except the trees, which stirred only when a gust of wind picked up. The thermometer read forty degrees below zero. There were no winter sports here, only winter survival.

For dinner, Charlotte had made Rivel soup. It was a concoction of doughy lumps floating in a milky goo. Michael rarely had a problem eating anything she made, but one look into the pot and his stomach turned. He had always been plagued with colds and excessive mucous, and what he saw floating in the pot looked like nothing more than what he blew out of his nose.

"Mommy, I can't eat that," he said, his stomach still churning.

"Why not?" she asked. "You can at least try it. It won't hurt you!"

He risked another glance into the pot just as an especially disgusting glob floated by. "I just can't," he said again.

"You *will* eat it and be thankful for it!" Carl roared.

When they had all been seated around the battered little table and the prayer offered, Charlotte ladled it out into their soup bowls. Michael saw Carl watching him like a hawk and knew he absolutely had to eat it. At the same time, he knew he simply could not eat it. He picked up his spoon and filled it with one of the less odious-looking globs, squeezed his eyes shut, and spooned it into his mouth. Horror of horrors, it was even slimier than it looked! *I gotta swallow it*, he thought, desperately trying manfully not to cry. He summoned all his courage and swallowed. It was about halfway down his throat when his stomach rebelled. He lurched to his feet and stumbled out the door, just as the horrible glob shot out of his mouth, with the former contents of his stomach, staining the snow a dirty brown.

Sick and humiliated, he slunk back inside in time to hear Charlotte remark to Carl that he must be sick. No more was said about him eating it, and he would never again try the stuff.

As the long cold winter dragged on, all the adventure of their new "apartment" wore off. The freezing cold nights were the worst, and the tight living quarters ran a close second. Carl, never blessed with patience, became even more short-tempered and rough. Although he at times displayed disrespect toward Charlotte, he was constantly watching for any real or imagined disrespect toward her by her small sons. When he observed any such violation, his reaction was swift and violent!

One evening during the supper conversation, Randy made a completely innocent remark to her that struck Carl as disrespectful. Instantly, his powerful hand shot out and flat-handed Randy across the left ear. Randy screamed as white hot pain from his broken ear-drum seared inside his head! He grabbed the sides of his head and pulled it down to his chest as he rocked from side, screaming and writhing in agony. Saliva drooled unnoticed from his mouth, as the rest of the family sat in stunned, horrified silence. Then, Carl Jr., at risk to himself, slid his chair over to the screaming Randy and gently tried to remove his hand from the wounded ear. Randy, nearly out of his mind in agony, could not stop clutching it.

Carl Jr. with incredible courage mumbled, "We learned in school to be really careful with our ears!"

Randy would never again hear properly out of that ear. Carl, of course, had no apology, no compassion; this was his family, and he was god!

When the storm finally passed, the skies cleared, and the sunshine was incredibly bright on the white snow. Carl scrounged up some large planks and nailed them in a V formation with a log chain fastened to the front of the V. Then, he harnessed the horses and hitched them to the contraption and dragged it up and down the driveway and down the hill to the barn. The V created a snow plow, pushing the snow off to both sides and creating a path between the banks. At some places, the snow was higher than the horses' bellies, causing them to bound through the drifts. All the boys were allowed to sit on the plow to add weight to keep it from floating over the drifts. It was a very jerky ride until the second or third pass when the horses could walk normally.

The road was closed for several days after the blizzard had ended. Finally, one day, a huge dump truck roared into view with an enormous V plow mounted on the front. The snow was so deep that the truck had to keep backing up and ramming the big drifts to make forward progress. They finally opened a path wide enough for one car to pass. The plowed banks were so high that you could only see the top of the truck. When cars went through the opened path, they were not visible at all since the snow in most places was at least twice as high as their roofs. It was great fun for the boys to sled down the hills and build a snowman. With the weather so cold though, they could only play outside for a short time and then had to go back inside and warm their hands, feet, and faces.

A few days later, it was back to school. Michael didn't enjoy school much except for the magic he found in the tattered old library books. They had the power to whisk him away to all sorts of interesting places and find adventure a little kid from the sticks could barely imagine. Someday, he vowed to himself that he would travel to all these places and see them firsthand. For now though, he had to put the book down and work on his tedious schoolwork.

CHRISTMAS VACATION

Christmas was coming. The Christmas spirit was in the air at the little Keefer's corner school. There would be a gift exchange among the students, as well as a school play, followed by a visit from Santa Claus. The Santa Claus thing was a bit odd for the Raptor boys, since their parents' religion stressed truth and honesty and didn't believe it was right to teach their children such fables even to entertain them. Miss Hart drilled the students for weeks on their lines for the school play. She tried hard to include each student with at least a couple lines. Her attempts to include Delilah Wickson, however, required every ounce of patience she possessed. Her first struggle was to get her to overcome her Marilyn Monroe complex every time she got the attention. Then, there was the issue of her quasi-incoherent speech. Miss Hart finally condensed her part down to one line that said, "My little bell rings out to say this is a happy Christmas Day." As she delivered this line, she was to hold a small bell aloft and gently tinkle it.

On the day of the celebration, the students exchanged gifts. No one in the community had the resources for expensive gifts, but Carl Jr. had gotten Delilah' brother Duncan's name and had managed to scrape up enough money to buy him a small pocketknife. He was rewarded with an impressive amount of appreciation, as Duncan went around proudly showing it off to the other kids, and Randy overheard him confiding in some of them that this is, "Just what he had wanted ever since he was a kid."

That evening, the parents trickled in from all over the community. The school desks had been pushed back, and the room was jammed with parents and families. The play went reasonably well with the usual amount of stage fright and forgotten lines. Finally, it was time for Delilah to give her line. She almost ran to the front of the makeshift stage and stood there a few long moments grinning like a lunatic. Then, she raised the little bell high above her head and jangled it like a fire alarm as she said, "My litto bell wings out to thay this is a happy kissie day!" Carl Jr. and Randy snickered, and even some of the adults tried to hide their grins. His brothers would tease Michael mercilessly for years to come about "his girlfriend" thinking it was a "happy kissie day"!

Then, there was a commotion at the back door, and in walked a giant of a man in a Santa Claus suit, carrying a bag of inexpensive gifts. He made a lot of deep-throated Ho Ho's, and when he joked with the children, he sounded just like Nate Rawson, but Michael was rather confused about the whole Santa Claus thing, so he just accepted his gift and stopped trying to figure it all out.

*****

Christmas vacation was fun, with lots of snow for sledding and, of course, lots of horseback riding. The horse cart Carl had built was used nearly every day in the summer and in the winter as well unless the snow was too deep. The boys enjoyed sledding and riding their sleds down the barn hill. On Christmas morning, there was a shiny new long toboggan propped up against the wall of the living room with Randy's name on it. It was from Pastor Randy because Randy Raptor had been named after him. Michael was too young to think much about it, but Carl Jr. was often hurt and even angered by the unfair favors Pastor Randy bestowed on his younger brother. Randy received gifts the Raptor children had never even seen. Not only had they never even seen a toboggan before, but also in years to come, Pastor Randy would shower him with such things as rare gold coins and all kinds of cool toys. Years later, Carl Jr. would remark to Michael, "For such a wise man of God, Pastor Randy sure didn't show much sensitivity to Randy's brothers."

After several days of sledding down and trudging back up the hill, the boys hit upon the idea of tying their sleds and the new toboggan behind the horses and letting them pull them around. It took a while for the horses to get used to the pressure of the rope on the saddle horns, but soon, they were flying down the snow-packed roads and across the fields.

There was, however, a price for Michael to pay for all this fun in the snow. His lungs had always been weak, and he was incredibly susceptible to colds and croup. Like the Wickson children, he suffered almost constantly from runny nose and mucous buildup. Unlike them, however, he kept his nose wiped clean. One night toward the end of Christmas vacation, he was having trouble breathing. Charlotte kept a close eye on him as he went up to bed. By now, they were moved back into the farmhouse, so at least he didn't have to sleep in the ice-cold garage; but sometime in the night, his bronchial tubes closed so tightly he could barely suck in any air at all. He woke in a panic and tried to scream for help, but all he could manage was a wheezing gasp. Fortunately, the noise and his thrashing were enough to wake Randy who was sharing the bed with him. Randy took one look at his terrified face and raced downstairs to get mommy. Charlotte felt an icy finger of fear touch her heart as she saw his desperate eyes in his face that was rapidly turning black! She snatched him up and carried him down to the kitchen where she lit a fire under a large teakettle. As the water came to a boil, she tried to clear the little boy's airways and calm him. She knew he was depleting precious oxygen by his panicked thrashings.

When the water was boiling hot, she sat him on a chair and placed the steaming kettle under the chair. Then, she threw a heavy blanket over his head, forming a steam tent. The steam rose to his head, giving him nearly instant relief as it cleared his airways. Young as he was, Michael would never forget that night and the terror of slowly suffocating as he struggled for air. His mother had saved his life. He would need the steam tent many more times in years to come, but never would he be as near death as that night!

When school resumed, he noticed many of the children with coughs and runny noses. The Raptors could not afford such luxuries as Kleenex or even handkerchiefs, so Michael learned to carry strips of rags in his pockets, torn from worn-out underwear or shirts. It seemed he was constantly blowing his nose, but he never allowed it to run down across his mouth and chin like the Wickson children. He marveled at how little it seemed to bother them. One day after recess, he heard an odd noise behind him and turned around to see Delilah reach her index finger up her nose and draw out a long green string of slimy goo. She slowly drew it out, her eyes crossing as she watched it carefully. When it was several inches out, and just about to break free, she extended her tongue and slurped the slimy mass into her mouth! Michael watched it all in mesmerized horror. He would see a lot of terribly gross things in his life, but nothing as disgusting as this!

In early March, the winter began to ease its iron grip on the land, and slowly, the days began to warm. Mornings and nights would still be very cold, but for a couple of hours in the early afternoon, the sun would shine and the snowbanks began to melt a bit. One day at lunch recess, Michael was sitting on the porch railing above the hand pump when he decided to jump down. It was only about a six-foot fall, but his feet went out from under him on the wet ice, and he landed on his chin. He felt terrific pain in his chin, and when he reached his hand to touch it, it came away sticky with blood. Miss Hart cleaned the wound and bandaged it for him, but it took weeks to heal. He would later discover that he had chipped the chin bone, leaving it jagged under the chin. He would have to be careful the rest of his life as the slightest bump under his chin would send the jagged chin bone through the scar tissue, making it bleed again.

Finally, the last day of school arrived. There were snacks and parties, and in the afternoon, the students cleared out their desks and stacked them neatly against the wall. This year end was different than any before. Although the children were not informed, the school district had decided that it would be more efficient to close the little school and bus the children to the schools in town. The last act Miss Hart performed before final closing was to lay all the library books out on a long table and allow the children to take turns choosing one at a time. Michael spied his two beloved books and was desperately afraid someone else would choose them before his turn came. But sure enough, when his turn came to choose, there they both were. He wished he could choose them both at once, but he chose *The Horse*

That Takes The Milk Around first and then sat on pins and needles with his eyes glued on *Flip And The Cows*. Miracle of miracles, when all the students had chosen again and it was his turn, it was still lying there. He snatched it off the table like the treasure it was, although by now he could almost quote it by heart. On the next round, he chose a very large and very tattered book called *Horses Now And Long Ago*, which told in detail many true stories of how horses had helped shape civilizations for nearly as long as man existed. It was several years before he finished reading all the stories in this book, and some were hard to understand because he couldn't visualize other civilizations. His only point of reference for visualization was the community where he had always lived and very occasional trips to nearby towns.

When the last book was chosen, the little schoolhouse was cleaned, and the final bell rang. No one was happier than Michael as he hiked the half-mile home with Randy and Carl Jr. Three whole months with no studies! He was certainly ready for the break.

RANDY

"Randy, you and Michael bring me some more boards," Carl Jr. ordered imperiously. "I'm gonna start building the shack." They were in the little aspen grove out behind the barn that they used every summer as their construction site.

"C'mon Michael," Randy muttered as he turned away to search for more old boards and nails to salvage from the tumbledown barn and garage.

"Why does he always hafta be the boss?" Michael grumbled when they were far enough away that Carl Jr. couldn't hear. Every summer, the boys would build a crude shack in the little grove of aspen trees behind the barn. The first shack was extremely crude, but each year, they got progressively better. There seemed to be plenty of old boards and nails around, and when it was time to build the new shack, they would tear the old one down and reuse those boards as well as more they would scavenge.

"When we get back, let's tell him we ain't gonna listen to him anymore," Randy suggested. Although he had never really thought about staging a rebellion, Michael thought this sounded like a fine plan.

They returned a short while later with a pitifully small supply of lumber. Carl Jr. looked at them in disbelief and yelled, "I told you to get some lumber, not two miserable boards!"

Randy looked at him calmly and said, "We decided you can get your own boards. You aren't our boss." Carl Jr. exploded like a grenade!

"If it wasn't for me, you guys wouldn't even know how to build anything!" he shouted. "And now you don't even want to do your part!"

"Who says our part is finding and carrying boards?" Randy asked. "We like to pound nails too."

"Yeah," Michael contributed. "We can do that as good as you!"

"Okay, just forget it," Carl Jr. shouted, hurling his hammer into the bushes, "We ain't gonna build no shack!" Carl Jr. had inherited his father's wild temper, and as he got older, it began to manifest itself more often and more forcibly. In years to come, he would often vent his anger and frustration by throwing a tool he was using accompanied by what he thought was a lionlike roar. He stormed up the hill toward the house.

"See," Randy commented to Michael. "I told you we don't hafta take orders from him!"

"But we won't have our shack this summer," Michael replied worriedly.

Randy's laugh was almost a snort. "He will be back down here by tomorrow. Just wait and see."

Sure enough, the next morning, the construction project was in full swing. Nobody mentioned any immediate need for additional lumber.

It was the first of what would become many years of Randy and Michael sticking together, and it felt rather good. Michael was still small enough to be intimidated by Carl Jr. who realized this and got a lot of mileage out of it.

*****

"Let's go riding," Randy suggested. "I need to work with Dusty." Michael needed no encouragement. He had graduated to a faster horse and couldn't get enough of the thrill of sitting astride and mastering the powerful animals. Dusty was still rather skittish about accepting the saddle and bridle, but Randy murmured soothingly and calmed him, while he eased the saddle onto his back and tightened the cinch strap. Michael held him by the halter, and Randy swung up smoothly into the saddle. Dusty pranced and hopped nervously, but soon, they were turning out of the barn lane and onto the gravel road. It was a long straight and flat stretch of road, and after a warmup trot, with Dusty was prancing and straining at the bit, Randy let him break into a canter. Michael was able to draw up alongside at this controlled pace.

"It doesn't matter how much rein I give him," Randy shouted over the drum roll of the horses' hooves. "He always wants to go faster!"

"Did you ever let him go as fast as he wanted to?" Michael asked.

"No," Randy replied. "'Cuz he has a problem spooking at things in the ditch, and if he did that at full speed, I don't think I could hang on."

"How about we ride in the woods across the road?" Michael suggested.

They slowed their mounts and turned them in to the shadowy trail through the huge swampy forest that bordered the north side of the farm. This forest was rather scary, even on horseback. They had never actually seen the bears or wildcats rumored to live in here, but sometimes at night, they could hear the screams of the big cats. Some of them sounded exactly like the scream of a woman, but much louder. The sound of those screams sent icy chills up the boys' spines and made them duck under the covers for the psychological safety they found there.

The other danger was the bottomless bogs these woods concealed. They were the swampy equivalent of quicksand, which would suck an incautious person or animal down, and the more they struggled, the farther they would sink until they disappeared completely under the slime-covered surface. Carl had often warned the boys to be careful to avoid the swampy areas and keep to higher ground.

About a half mile into the forest, the trail ended, and they began to pick their way around trees, fallen logs, and brushy areas. It became more tangled as they got in deeper, and soon, it became a matter of finding enough open space for a horse and rider to pass. As they rode, they forgot all about the passing of time and their direction of travel with all their concentration focused on finding passageways. They crossed a small stream and paused to let their horses drink their fill and grab a few mouthfuls of the grass growing close by. `

Suddenly, a thought jolted Michael back to reality! "Randy, do you know where we are?" he asked tremulously.

Randy looked startled. He thought for a long moment and then admitted, "No, I have no idea. I wasn't paying attention."

They hastily remounted and headed back the way they had come, but an hour later, they arrived at the very same spot where they had watered their horses. They were lost! Michael was scared and felt like crying, but somehow, it didn't seem right to cry on horseback. It was a feeling that would follow him all his life, and although he would sort out all kinds of powerful emotions on horseback, he would never cry while he was riding. Although Randy was only a year and a half older, they both knew he would take the lead in extracting them from the dark clutches of this forest.

"Well," he said finally. "Daddy says that horses can always find their way home, so we have to stop steering them and let them find their way back. I have to hold Dusty back, or he'll take off like a wild deer, so you go first and leave the reins loose on your horse, and we will follow."

Michael had heard Carl say that many times as well, but he had never really believed it. How could horses be smarter than people? But they were out of options, so he nudged his horse past Randy and Dusty and let the reins loose. As the minutes turned into hours, he became more and more convinced that they would be trapped in these woods all night. Through the occasional openings in the canopy above, he could see the sun was on its way down, and the woods were getting spookier. His stomach clenched as he thought of the terrible wildcats that roamed these woods. His eyes involuntarily flickered up to the treetops ahead. The cougars had a vicious habit of crouching in the lower tree branches and dropping silently on their victim as it passed beneath. The thought of one of those deadly creatures dropping on him made his small body shiver with fright! He thought he probably should pray for their safety, but wasn't real sure that helped. He had been taught from babyhood that praying would solve problems for you, but he had performed a number of situational tests on that theory, and the results had been at best, inconclusive!

And suddenly, the underbrush thinned, and his horse was on the forest trail they had come in on. He turned and saw the relief on Randy's face. "Wow!" Randy exclaimed. "These horses really do know their way back home!"

Yup, Michael thought, *that theory works*. The other one, however, would require more testing.

They turned their horses west on the gravel road leading back to the farm. Michael nudged his horse into a gallop and thrilled to the feel of the wind on his face from the running horse. Suddenly, a buckskin blur passed him on the left side, and he realized that Dusty was ready to get home. He watched with admiration tinged with awe as the buckskin horse shot past and headed for the barnyard gate with huge ground-eating bounds. He recalled Carl telling them at the dinner table one day that he had ridden up close to a very tired deer one morning and decided to try to catch it. His horse hadn't been fast enough, but Carl had remarked that he was sure if he had been riding Dusty, he could have caught him. Watching the horse and rider thunder toward home now, Michael had no doubt that he could have kept up with the deer.

Dusty had grown into a beautiful, well-formed horse, and in the summer, his coat turned a yellowish cream color set off by a black mane and tail. Dusty's tail would forever be a source of irritation to Randy. The horses would pick up cockleburs in their manes and tails, and Carl had a bad habit of just cutting the hair off and letting it grow back in. The boys hated the looks of horses with their manes or tails cut short. Michael even struggled to save the forelocks, the hair that grew at the front of the mane and dropped down over their foreheads. Carl with his total lack of appreciation for class or aesthetics never took the time to clean out the burrs. He just cut the hair off.

What had really gotten to Randy though was the time when his father took the shears to Dusty's tail and cut too close to the stump. This had the effect of "docking" the tail, which kept the long beautiful hair from growing back. Dusty would go through life with a wispy stump for where his long black beautiful tail had once been. He was still, however, a very handsome horse.

HORSEPOWER AND TRACTORS

It was haying time again. The barnyard was full of worn and battered haying machinery in various stages of repair and maintenance. Preventive maintenance was a concept that got very little focus on the Raptor farm. Grandpa's machinery was in slightly better condition, but breakdowns were common since worn parts and bearings usually got replaced only after they had given their very last minute of usefulness. The power to operate and propel the antiquated machinery was provided by a combination of worn-out tractors and horse teams. Driving the horses was fun for the boys for the first year or two; then, they longed for the day they could graduate to the tractors. There were three old two-cylinder model John Deere tractors.

The smallest was a model H that produced over twelve horsepower and was used only for light work such as raking hay or pulling light wagons or machinery. It boasted a maximum road speed of over seven miles per hour.

The main workhorse was the model A. At twenty-six horsepower, it could pull a plow or disk and had a dizzying road speed of twelve miles per hour!

Then, there was the huge, clumsy Model D. The boys saw it as a powerful machine. It only produced twenty-five horsepower, but its great weight and low gearing made it good for plowing or the other heavy duty applications. The problem with the D was that it had a top road speed of approximately four miles per hour. The tires were huge and the sheet metal fenders flared wide enough for several small boys to sit between the incredibly uncomfortable seat and the wheels.

Michael liked to stand beside the seat and look forward over the huge rounded cowling covering the engine. The tractor made deep uneven *pop pop* popping sounds like huge firecrackers exploding at random intervals.

There were two problems associated with using the tractors instead of horse teams. One was the cost of the gas to run them. Although gasoline was relatively cheap, it still drained scarce cash resources.

The other was the hassle of starting the engines. Electric starters were still a thing of the future when these tractors were manufactured, and they needed to be started by hand. Each tractor had a large cast iron flywheel on the left side and a power pulley on the right side. The pulley was used to power stationary machinery with a wide flat belt mounted between the tractor pulley and a pulley on the machine.

The flywheel was used to keep the engine turning through its cycles to provide the power to the transmission. To start the tractor, it was necessary to open a pressure relief valve on either side of the engine and then manually spin the flywheel, much like pilots used to spin their airplane propellers to start their engines. It might require only one or two spins, or it might not start at all, depending on the condition of the engine, how long since it had been run, and the weather. Starting these tractors in the winter was a serious challenge. A common trick was to prewarm the engine by placing a bucket of hot coals under it. This created the risk of oil or fuel dripping from the ancient engines into the bucket of coals and igniting a fire that would instantly spread to the engine and burn the machine to a charred hulk.

Carl kept the tractors parked on a hill and attempted to pop-start them by rolling them down the hill. If that failed, he would crank on the flywheel until he was frustrated enough to spew invectives not lawful to be uttered in the Raptor household and then, as a last resort, harness a team of horses to pull it until it would start.

This year Carl had decreed that Michael would be taking over the dump rake. It sounded exciting to Michael, and he caught on fast to the simple operation of the machine. The dump rake was a steel contraption about ten feet wide with large curved tines the entire width, which scooped up the mown hay. At each side was a large steel wheel with studs to bite into the ground for traction. At the center of the machine was a steel seat for the operator, directly behind the long tongue extending forward between the two horses pulling it. When the curved tines were full of hay, the operator would step on a steel foot pedal and engage a tripping mechanism powered by the wheels that would raise the tines, dumping the collected hay on a pile about two feet high by ten feet wide. The forks would immediately descend again, and this procedure would be repeated all the way across the field. On the way back, the operator would empty the forks at the exact same place as the last trip, making the row twenty feet long. The pattern would be maintained all the way across the field, creating windrows for the hay loader to collect.

Michael was sure the job would be fun, and it was—for about a day and a half. But soon, the dull repetition became tedious beyond description. The only noise were the creaks and jangle of horse harness and the regular ka-chunk of the rake dumping. His eyelids got heavy and his operation of the dump rake more sluggish. It was important to dump the rake at the correct time to make nice straight rows, and this required constant vigilance, since the pedal needed to be tripped every few minutes. Small as he was, his vision was partially blocked by the huge rumps of the draft horses directly in front of him. There was also the hypnotic effect of the fly netting continually swishing to the rhythm of the horses' steps. Michael found the netting rather fascinating. It was a loosely woven net of thin leather strips that was laid over the horses' harness covering their backs and rumps. The motion of the moving horses kept the net in motion, discouraging the horseflies, deerflies, bees, and assorted other little winged nasties from landing long enough to do their evil deeds.

It was always a relief to see the rider coming to announce that dinner was ready. In this community, the morning meal was breakfast, the noon meal was dinner, and the evening meal, supper. The Raptor boys found it strange when they visited other communities where they called the evening meal dinner. Michael was pretty sure the correct name for it was supper. After all, the Bible says Jesus served his disciples supper, not dinner!

Michael unhitched the team from the rake and crawled on the back of the largest mare for the trip back to the barn. Carl had said that they were going to pick up hay at Rat Lake in the afternoon, so the raking was finished for the day. The day had started out very warm and was getting progressively hotter as the day wore on. It was good weather for drying hay but very hard on people and horses.

Arriving back at the barn, he tied the team to a manger and removed their bridles so they could chomp some hay during dinner. He would water them after lunch when they were cooled down. Carl had drilled into them at a very young age that you never give a hot horse water and then let them stand. Many a good horse had developed serious cramps and died from the resulting colic.

After lunch, another team of horses was harnessed to a hay wagon, and Michael and Randy climbed aboard, while Carl drove. Carl Jr. who had the most seniority rode one of the team Michael had been using, and they all headed down the road to grandpa's farm. There, they picked up Uncle Rusty and grandpa's team and wagon. Grandpa had already delivered the clumsy hay loader to the field, so the little convoy set out. It was approximately five miles to the end of the gravel road and then several miles into the forest on an old logging trail. The forest was dark and much cooler with the trail almost completely shaded by the huge trees on both sides whose branches commingled above to form a thick canopy. It was rather spooky. Michael was glad that the Indians all lived in town now, so they didn't need to worry about getting attacked and savaged by them. But it bothered him a little that Pastor Randy hadn't given any indication as to where and how the Catholics lived. Might this be where they skulked, waiting for their hapless victims? He thought it over and then decided that would be unlikely. The cooler air in here felt good, but the biting flies were terrible. Who would want to live where they were constantly being bitten by huge flies? It was a relief to finally burst out of the forest and into a small meadow.

The heat hit again like a hammer blow. The meadow was surrounded by thick trees and vegetation, which allowed for no breeze, and the humidity was almost unbearable. The hay loader was hitched behind the first wagon, and Carl Jr. drove the team, while Carl stacked the hay on the wagon. Randy had been left to help grandpa, so Michael and Uncle Rusty were given the task of straightening up the windrows with pitchforks. As the sweat poured from their bodies, their thirst became intense. No one had thought to bring drinking water since the plan had been to load all the hay on the three wagons and all head back to grandpa's farm. It wasn't long until Uncle Rusty was grumbling about the heat, the work, and whatever else he could think of to complain about. Michael had to agree on one point; he too was terribly thirsty.

They saw it at the same time, a small mud puddle from a passing shower the night before.

"Can we drink some of that?" Michael inquired hesitantly.

Without a word, Uncle Rusty went to his stomach on the ground and began to suck up the putrid brown liquid. Michael joined him moments later. The muddy water was thick and tasted rather sweet. It did not quench his thirst well, but the moisture felt good in his dry mouth. He could only hope that the tiny wigglers in the puddle managed to avoid getting sucked in with the murky water.

"Man, that stuff isn't good at all!" Uncle Rusty remarked, and then a smile spread across his handsome face. "Kinda cool though," he said. "We drank out of a mud puddle!"

Michael couldn't help grinning along. This was one of Uncle Rusty's traits that girls found irresistible; he wasn't afraid to try anything, and he never could see the need for living by other people's rules. While he had to endure a never-ending string of consequences for breaking rules, he found life much more interesting living where what would years later come to be known as "outside the box." The need to live on the edge would cause him incredible suffering and bring him within a whisker's breadth of death several times in the course of his life, but it was how he chose to live.

Michael pondered this as he lay in bed that night. He would like so much to be like Uncle Rusty that way. He seemed to be afraid of absolutely nothing, while Michael was afraid of almost everything, like the night thing. He feared to fall asleep each night for fear It would take control of him again! Although Charlotte had several times asked him to describe It, he could find no way to put It in words. It was referred to in the family as his "nightmares." He was the only one in the family who suffered from them, so he received little sympathy or understanding, but they were as real as life itself—as real as mommy and daddy and his brothers, as real as the house and the barn, and as real as Laddie!

PAL

It was Saturday, and Carl had been gone most of the day. He had gone to pick up Nate Rawson to go look at some horses. Charlotte knew that when Carl and Nate were together with horses, there was no telling when she would see him again. The boys were fast asleep in their beds when Carl's car chugged up the driveway, followed by an ancient pickup hauling a small pinto. The little horse was crosstied in the pickup bed's crude wooden rack. He was a little black and white beauty, and for the price of twenty-five dollars plus two dollars for delivery, Carl had been unable to resist buying the little stallion. He had been uneasy the whole way home because the man hauling him was either drunk or nearly so and had weaved and swerved the whole way, nearly ditching the truck several times. Carl and Nate had been amazed how the little horse had kept on his feet on the bed of the swaying and pitching machine!

The boys were surprised to see the little horse in the corral the next morning. He was wild and had never been tamed or broken to ride, which was not considered a big obstacle in this family. The big surprise was beside Michael's breakfast plate in the form of a note that stated that the new horse belonged to him! He could hardly eat his breakfast, and Charlotte allowed him to skip the dishwashing to go be with his new prize.

Outside, he looked the little horse over with new eyes—finally, a horse of his own. He decided to name him "Pal." The little horse watched him warily as he approached. He was too wild to touch, and Michael kept carefully out of range of his hind legs. He had seen the nimble Laddie nearly get clipped by a lightning-fast kick from the little pinto, and he had no desire to be his next target.

105

Carl went to work on the little horse later that morning. The training method of gentling horses and interacting with them was still many years away. The normal method of training was to subdue them and punish their wrongdoing until they learned to be compliant and obedient subjects. It was very similar to the normal method of child-rearing.

As the weeks rolled by, Carl was becoming frustrated by the stubbornness of the little animal. He had managed to ride him a few times, but each ride was a battle of wills and required tremendous power on the reins to control his head. He had what was known as a "hard mouth," meaning that he did not respond to the pressure of a bit in his mouth. He would break into a full gallop, and Carl could only stop him by sawing on the reins, meaning he would pull with all his strength on first one reign and then the other, pulling the horse's head from side to side to slow him. They would come back from training sessions with blood dripping from the little horse's mouth, but Michael noted that the proud fire in the little horse's dark eyes was never diminished. He was secretly proud of that. Every person or animal under his father's control had to be broken and submissive. His mother and his horse would be the only two exceptions!

One beautiful Saturday morning, Nate and Kermit Rawson came by to help geld the two newest horses, Dusty and Pal. Grandpa and Uncle Rusty came over to help, and the boys watched in fascination. The men threw Dusty to the ground and stretched out his legs with ropes. Then, Nate took a tool resembling a huge pliers with two foot-long wooden handles and crushed the life-carrying tubes in his groin. There was no anesthetic available, and Dusty first screamed and then let out a long, hideous groan of pure agony as his ability to sire colts was destroyed forever. Michael and Randy found the whole affair horrific and disturbing.

When it was over, the men helped Dusty to his feet where he stood swaying and trembling. Pal was next. Although he was smaller than Dusty, he fought the men like a cornered demon! But finally, he was down, and his legs secured with ropes. Michael watched numbly as Nate applied the tongs to his little horse. Pal's small body went rigid and broke out in instant sweat, but there was no scream from him. He would never be completely broken by men, and only a muffled, gurgling groan escaped him as his maleness was destroyed. Michael was tremendously proud of him. He wished so badly that he could find just a small fraction of the courage to face life that his little horse had in spades!

In a few days, the young horses had recovered from the ordeal and were useable again. Carl had not yet allowed Michael to ride Pal on the road because he did not have enough strength to control his hard mouth. Michael either had to ride in the corral or suffer the ignominy of being tethered to another horse during a ride.

This changed one day when Carl returned from an auction sale in the community with a special bit for Pal's bridle. Instead of a steel bar running through the mouth, it consisted of two twisted smaller bars that resembled oversized fence wire without the barbs. The bits were spliced at two different places inside the mouth creating a scissoring effect. When gently applied, it would be harmless, but it gave the rider the ability to project an unlimited amount of pressure and pain to a hardmouthed horse. It also eliminated the ability for the horse to seize the bit in his teeth, totally wresting all control from the rider. This had been one of Pal's favorite tricks. He would grab the bit in his teeth and take off like the wind. His rider would usually end up in the dust. Michael had learned to jump off quickly when this happened. It was much better to hit the ground before the horse was at a full gallop. The little horse was fast. Someone had once followed him at a full gallop and clocked his speed at thirty-five miles per hour. Michael would be unloaded at that speed more times than he could remember! But he didn't hold it against Pal. Their relationship often became a test of wits, which they both seemed to enjoy. He would never be a horse you could use for a leisurely ride on a calm day. He always vibrated and danced with energy, forcing his rider to be constantly tuned to his body language for unexpected tricks.

Michael learned to stay tuned to his ears especially. If they were turned back toward him and somewhat relaxed, he knew that there were no devious plans being hatched in the little black-and-white head. When the ears were alert and focusing on various objects around them, he was looking for some excuse to make life more exciting.

When the ears were erect and focused forward, Michael knew that it was nearly showtime and would try to guess at what would trigger the coming eruption! Bad things happened to Pal's riders who were not vigilant at such times. The little horse could move at the speed of a striking snake, bucking and twisting sideways, and the unsuspecting rider would find himself lying on the ground, watching a little black-and-white rump disappearing in the distance. If he was lucky, someone would see the riderless horse appear in the barnyard and come to pick him up, but usually, it was a long walk home.

Pal also managed to distinguish himself in the harness when Carl decided to hitch him beside one of the workhorses. It wasn't that he was needed for a workhorse, but Carl just liked all the horses to be useable for anything. Dusty had taken to the harness calmly, but soon proved to be rather worthless at helping to pull heavy loads. Pal seemed determined to take it one step better. He remained fairly calm during the harnessing and hitching process, but when Carl picked up the lines and clucked the horses into action, Pal exploded forward, snapping the heavy traces hitching him to the wagon. Carl, who had spent hours customizing a harness to make it small enough to fit him, was exasperated. He unharnessed him and repaired the broken trace and then rehitched him to the wagon.

This time, he held back a few seconds and then made another powerful leap forward, snapping a trace again like it had been a piece of string. He was a powerful little horse and could pull a surprising amount of weight, but he never got over his hobby of breaking traces. It seemed that he broke more traces than all the other horses combined, and eventually, Carl stopped trying to use him as a pulling horse. Score another round for the proud little horse with the unbroken spirit!

BRINGING HOME
THE COWS

Charlotte sipped her morning coffee deep in thought. "Have you thought this through carefully?" she asked Carl.

"Yes," he replied. "I've been considering it for a couple months now. Dad thinks it might be a good idea too, since it would allow me to be home all the time."

Charlotte sat in thoughtful silence. It was Pastor Randy who had found the mason jobs in Rango and was providing Carl and his father with plastering jobs. The cash had been ever so welcome, but they had been renting a damp, chilly basement for sleeping, and over time, the dampness had begun to affect Carl. The onset of arthritis had him using pain pills more and more frequently. There were really some very good reasons for him to alter his career.

"Yes," she said thoughtfully. "That would really be good for the family, but borrowing money to buy a whole herd of milk cows, that's kinda scary!"

"I checked with the bank," Carl said. "And they are willing to lend us the money for a herd of twenty-three cows I found for sale from a farmer who is retiring. I also checked with the creamery about selling milk instead of cream, and they will come and pick it up for that many cows."

"Where is this farm where the cows are, and how will you get them here?" she asked, still not totally convinced.

"It's only thirteen miles," Carl replied. "We will get the folks to help us and drive them cross-country. We can do it in a day!"

"Well, it's okay with me if you're sure it will pay," Charlotte said. "It would be really nice to have a man around all the time."

*****

"We're all going to bed early tonight," Charlotte announced after supper the next Friday night. "We have a big day tomorrow bringing those cows home."

Michael could hardly contain his excitement. They were going to have a real genuine cattle drive, like the ones he read about in the Zane Grey books. Sure, this one would be through forests and swamps instead of the dusty plains of the Wild West, but it would be fun.

Early morning found the Raptor men in the corral saddling and bridling every available horse. Grandpa, Uncle Rusty, and Aunt Leola were going to help too, so they were short one horse.

"Leola and Michael can trade off walking," Carl decided.

This pronouncement hit Michael like a hammer. He could see Aunt Leola was not pleased either. Here, he finally had his own horse, and now, he had to share him on the only cattle drive he would ever participate in! But he knew better than to object. Grandma followed the riders in grandpa's old Ford taking Aunt Leola and little Johnny with her. Michael was allowed to ride all the way to the farm where they would be picking up the cows, but would have to take turns walking on the way back when the cows were being herded through the woods. A few hours later, they rode into the farmyard. It was a typical reservation-style farm with an unpainted clapboard house with sagging doors and broken windows. The yard was overgrown with tangled weeds and vines and strewn with broken-down cars, machinery, and an assortment of other junk. The barnyard was a sight to behold as well. The tumbledown barn looked unsafe to even enter, and the fences were rotting with more barbed wire on the ground than on the posts.

"There's the herd," Carl remarked to grandpa, with a note of pride in his voice. Grandpa looked a bit dubious as he inspected the herd. The cows showed mostly Holstein breeding with a broad assortment of other breeds mixed in. They were not the gentle moo cows depicted in storybooks. Many of them were younger and were as frisky as the deer in the surrounding forest. One of them was especially crazy and would make the trip home very interesting indeed.

With the purchase finalized, the cows were driven out onto the lane leading to the gravel road. Some of the trip home would be on the road, but much of it would be cross-country to save miles. It soon became obvious that the walkers would be of limited use. The heifers in the bunch gave the horses a run for their money, and the walkers became runners just to keep up with the herd. Carl, who had trained a young sorrel gelding to replace Patsy, was a blur of motion. He was a superb horseman and rode like an extension of the animal under him, galloping, wheeling, and twisting to keep the cattle bunched and on the road. Carl Jr. was doing well on his filly as well. Grandpa didn't even try to keep up with the fancy riding; he just rode "drag" behind the herd with the walkers. Uncle Rusty was a good rider, but unless there were girls there to impress, he just didn't see the need to exert himself. Randy and Michael filled in as best they could to keep the herd bunched and moving. But it seemed Aunt Leola was constantly demanding her turn to ride Pal, and Michael spent a great deal of time on foot.

By the end of the first hour, the cattle were trailing fairly well. They left the gravel road and cut across fields, woods, and meadows, startling deer, coons, squirrels, and an occasional porcupine. They crossed a swamp and a couple shallow streams. The crazy cow kept Carl on his toes all the time. About the time the herd would be calm and sedate, she would bellow and bolt as if someone had poked her with a sharp stick. That would excite some of the others, and the show was on again. The riders enjoyed chasing them down in an open field where their mounts' superior speed gave them the advantage. They would swoop around the bolting cow at a full gallop and force her to reconsider her error in judgment as she was pushed back to the herd.

The crazy cow and some of her cohorts soon caught on that they had more success taking off in the woods. It was much easier for a young cow to charge full speed through the woods than a horse and rider. The rider had to constantly protect himself from getting his legs crushed between the horse and a tree trunk while at the same time guarding against low-hanging tree limbs that would slash his face and body or even sweep him off the running horse. They would have to follow the cow until she slowed down and then get around her and turn her back in the proper direction.

After several more hours, everyone was getting weary, and the horses were soaking with sweat. Michael and Aunt Leona had worked out a system of trading off walking and riding Pal. Her turn had just ended. Michael mounted and joined the other riders when the herd broke out onto the gravel road leading to the farm. Pastor Oliver and his children were sitting in his car on the road to offer their help on the rest of the drive. Michael and Pal were still in the woods when he heard Aunt Leona's urgent voice calling his name.

"Michael, Michael, come here," her voice was low and insistent. Michael turned back to where she was concealed in some bushes. "Let me have Pal," she demanded.

"No!" he responded. "You just had your turn!"

"Just let me have him for a few minutes, and you can have him the rest of the way home," she insisted. He was puzzled by her strange behavior, but was not about to pass up an opportunity like this. He swung down, and she scrambled hastily into the saddle. Then, she rode out of the bushes and onto the road. When she saw Danny looking her way, she kicked the little horse into a fast run and galloped past their car. A hundred yards down the road, she turned him around and galloped back past the car and into the woods. Safely concealed in the bushes again, she returned the horse to her incredulous nephew who had just figured out what she was doing, showing off for Danny Mason. He mounted Pal, then turned, and treated her to a flat stare of disbelief. Young as he was, he really didn't understand girls at all, but he was pretty sure that this was the dumbest thing he had ever seen!

An hour later, all the cows had been successfully herded into the barnyard, and it was time to milk them. The milking was a chaotic mess. The only existing facility was the short row of tie stalls in the little barn, making it necessary to milk a small batch of cows and then turn them out and milk another small batch until they had all been milked. As a rule, cows adapt well to routines, but these cows were confused and not used to being overly cooperative even on their best behavior. The milking machines were the type that hung under the cow's belly, suspended by a strap over her back.

When the cow was finished, the lid would be removed from the "milker" and the contents poured into a straining hopper sitting atop a ten-gallon galvanized metal milk can. The cans had a handle on each side near the neck where it tapered down to the removable lid. When the can was full, the strainer would be transferred to an empty can and the lid wedged onto the top of the full can. The can would then be carried to a large water tank where the water would cool the milk to keep it from spoiling. The old cream separator was retired to a dusty corner of the garage. It would not be missed, especially since it was so difficult and time-consuming to clean due to all the little plates and parts that had to be dismantled every time it was properly cleaned. The Raptor dairy farm had officially been taken to the next level.

FIRECRACKERS

The new cow herd took the Raptor farm to a whole new phase. Carl had borrowed enough extra money to build an addition to the barn to house the cows in the winter. He had also planted more corn, which needed to be cultivated. The corn cultivator was a horse-drawn machine with steel wheels and a steel seat for the operator. Operating this machine was a job only Carl could do due to its exacting nature. The cultivator had three sets of spades separated by two gaps for the corn rows to pass through. The spades, which could be raised and lowered from the operator's seat, tore up the ground between the rows of corn, rooting out the weeds and keeping the corn roots growing down toward the ground moisture. It was pulled by a team of two horses that had to be carefully guided so that each horse walked between the corn rows without stepping on the corn and crushing the plants. Any amount of swerving would cause the corn shoots to be crushed by the big hooves of the horses or ripped out by the cultivator spades. It was a slow and tedious process, but it was the only affordable way to keep the weeds from robbing nutrition from the soil and choking out the corn.

*****

Pastor Randy, grandpa, and Carl had finally completed their last mason job in Rango. The pay had been good, but it was a time when labor unions were on the rise, and contractors who refused to join were being harassed. One especially persistent union thug had been harassing them for months and was beginning to threaten them with violence if they didn't join. This was particularly galling to a huge, powerful Indian on the crew named Merno. He simply couldn't understand why they didn't run the guy off once and for all. One morning, the crew was plastering the upstairs of a new house when the union organizer came storming into the house. He shouted up the stairs for them to come down and talk, at which Pastor Randy calmly turned to Merno and said in a voice that clearly carried down to the organizer.

"Merno, you go down and take care of him."

The slightly built union man took one look at the huge, menacing Indian descending the stairs and made a hasty retreat, never to be heard from again.

Later, Grandpa asked Pastor Randy, "Exactly what did you expect Merno to do with him?"

Pastor Randy laughed and said, "I don't know, but he looked mighty important going down those stairs!"

On his final trip home from Rango, instead of bringing the boys a toy back with him, Carl had brought something far more fun and exciting—firecrackers! He didn't allow the boys to set them off by themselves, but they had great sport helping him set them off around the farm. Carl especially got a kick out of setting them off behind Charlotte when she wasn't looking. She tolerated it for a while and then decided to retaliate. When he wasn't looking, she helped herself to several firecrackers from the pack and carried them around in her apron pocket with some matches, looking for an opportunity. The opportunity presented itself one morning when she was helping him hitch the team to the corn cultivator.

He was hitched up and had just climbed up onto the metal seat when he found it necessary to lean forward and adjust the cultivator settings. As his rear end left the cultivator seat, Charlotte who was standing behind him snatched a firecracker from one apron pocked and lit the fuse with a match from the other pocked, tossing it hissing onto the now-empty cultivator seat, only seconds before he sat back down. Instead of the expected crack of the firecracker, there was a howl of pain from Carl as the burning fuse set the seat of his pants on fire! He leaped from the cultivator, swatting at his behind, still not understanding what was biting him back there. Charlotte was doubled over with laughter, while Carl Jr. looked on in amazement. If he had pulled a stunt like that, he would have gotten his butt blistered but good. His mother however had finally evened the score. The season of the firecracker passed that day from the Raptor farm, never to return.

*****

The new cows proved to be a disappointment. Many of them were dry, and some hadn't been bred back, and Carl had no bull to service them. He would need to borrow a bull from a neighbor ten miles away. The neighbor had just bought the bull and was willing to share him. The problem was he was wild and mean! He said that he would put a ring in his nose attached to a short chain to make him more manageable. Before he could accomplish this however, the bull broke through the barnyard fence and vanished into the surrounding forest.

He called around to the neighbors to come and help him find the missing bull. Early one morning, a posse of mounted men and dogs spread out to search an area about six miles from his farm where he had been spotted. Some of the children were allowed to trail along behind but were ordered not to get close to the bull; he was a wild and dangerous animal. The dogs picked up the scent, and the riders soon had the bull on the run. But this bull was much more wily than the herd of cows had been. He avoided open meadows and roads and ran through the brushiest and swampiest areas in the huge forest. The dogs were able to keep up with him, but the mounted men only got occasional glimpses of the reddish brown animal tearing through the trees like a young moose. They finally worked out a strategy of fanning out around him and forcing his flight path toward the farm. As the hours passed, men and horses began to wear down, and even the dogs were panting. But they were getting closer to the farm and were seeing more and more of the bull. Finally, several riders closed in hard behind him and forced him onto the gravel road. Other riders joined them, and together, they were able to drive him up the lane toward the man's barn. They managed to surround him, and several ropes snaked out and settled around his huge neck. The powerful beast put up a valiant fight, but more ropes captured his legs, which were yanked out from under him, and he fell heavily to the ground, panting with exhaustion, but still as belligerent as when he had first escaped. With the animal subdued, the farmer approached with the nose ring and chain. The nose ring was approximately three inches in diameter and opened on a hinge. The opened ends were sharp enabling them to pierce the cartilage inside the bull's nose; then, they closed together and were fastened by a tiny screw. The farmer had pierced the nose and was closing the ring when someone remarked, "Hey, he stopped breathing!"

The men stepped back in stunned silence. After giving them the chase of their lives, the mighty beast had died the instant the ring had pierced his nose! None of them had ever witnessed anything like this before. It seemed he had chosen death over domesticity! The farmer who owned him took the loss stoically. "Well," he commented. "I guess we have our winter's supply of meat."

The cow herd turned out to be a big disappointment. Many of them had an infectious condition called mastitis and permanently lost the ability to produce milk in one or even two of their four udder quarters. Then, there was the constant fight with the wild cow that they had named Fireball. She ran and jumped like a deer and would burst through a fence like it wasn't even there. Carl had constructed a wooden corral beside the barn to hold the herd, while they awaited their turn for milking. He was forced to keep building the rails higher and higher to keep her from jumping over and escaping. Finally, it was over six feet high, and Carl was sure he had her contained. One evening at milking time, she waited until the corral was almost cleared of cows and then took a running start and made a flying leap over the fence. But this time, she barely got her front legs over, and hung on the top rail for a few seconds, balancing on her belly until the rail broke under her weight, and she toppled and slid down the outside and galloped away to the big pasture.

The barn was far too small for the old cows plus the new herd, so Carl had gotten creative. He had heard of the new concept called milking parlors where they would build a row of four enclosures just large enough for one cow, end to end with a gate into and out of each pen. A batch of cows would be channeled in the back door from the corral, milked, and then let out the front door and back to the pasture, after which a new batch would be ushered in; and the cycle would be repeated until all were milked.

Carl's parlor had some serious design flaws however. While Carl was long on imagination, he had always been short on craftsmanship. Properly constructed parlor pen floors were made of grooved concrete to ensure traction for the cows entering and exiting. They were also elevated approximately four feet above the floor where the people stood to milk them, this saving them from having to constantly work doubled over and reaching under the cow.

Carl's parlor pen floors were about twelve inches high and constructed of wood. Thus, not only did the operator have to work doubled over, but also the cows would slip and slide and often fall heavily on the boards, which became slimy and slick from cow waste. There was also the matter of the manure and urine dropping through the boards into the small space below, which was extremely difficult to clean out. The design was a disaster, but there was no money to rebuild it so that was how it was used.

Charlotte made a game of naming the cows with the boys' help. One large, ancient creature was given the regal name of Queen Liz, taken out of a book she had read to the children. She was the kinetic opposite of Fireball, but would in the course of events be responsible for instigating a highly unusual crisis on the farm. The current crisis of the escaping Fireball was managed by keeping a horse saddled and tied to the corral during chores to run her down and drive her back to surrender her tiny offering of milk, where she would kick and struggle through every milking. She suffered many a bad fall on the slimy parlor floorboards, but would always gallop back out to pasture afterward.

Highway Construction

Michael was running for his life! He wasn't totally sure why he was marked for death, but he knew it would be at the hands of the insanely furious man just a few steps behind who was running with his hands outstretched toward him, the fingers crooked like the talons of a hawk he had seen in a picture.

Carl Jr. and Randy had been playing in the gravel on the drive with little cars and trucks when Michael had wandered up to watch. As they pushed their cars aimlessly around, he was suddenly seized by inspiration.

"Hey!" he said. "You guys need some roads. I'll make you some."

He ran to the garage and retrieved a heavy crowbar with a flat end that he poked to the ground where they were playing and began to drag it, creating a track in the gravel roughly resembling a road. His efforts were not appreciated however, and they told him to get that thing out of there and leave them alone.

He would always be unclear as to just what his father had seen or heard that set off the volcanic anger in him, but out the corner of his eye, he saw the furious man striding toward him with cold fire burning in the slate-gray eyes. One look at the twisted face and the protruding lower teeth grinding his upper lip, and something in Michael knew in his heart that he would not survive this beating! For the first and only time in his life, he ran from his father. He raced into the house, hoping to find his mother, but the house was empty.

There was no sign of Carl for a few minutes, and he had just begun daring to hope he had escaped when he heard the screech of the porch door and the heavy tread of a large man coming fast. Like a deer, he raced toward the stair steps, and then his panicked brain registered that the upstairs would be a trap with no exit. The house was built around the stairways up and down, enabling him to circle the stairs indefinitely. There was only one thought in his mind as he raced around the stairways—if his father got his hands on him, he would beat him to death! Then, he realized that he was actually out-running his father, and a flicker of hope kindled in his fear-numbed brain. Suddenly, as he passed the downstairs doorway, a powerful arm shot out and seized him, jerking him almost off his feet. His father had ambushed him and was now dragging him down into the cellar, shaking with uncontrolled rage.

This time, there was no command to strip. Carl slammed him across his knee and ripped his pants and shorts down in one mighty jerk. Michael shrieked in terror and pleaded for mercy.

"I'll never do it again!" he pleaded, not sure what "it" was. "I'll be good! I'll be good! I'll be good!"

But Carl wasn't interested in whether his son would be good or not. It was judgment time. Michael twisted his terror-stricken face around toward his father and saw something that turned his heart into a lump of ice. The reason for his brief reprieve earlier was now clear. Carl had made a fast trip to the barn to retrieve the cattle prod!

He rammed the prod's steel electrodes into the naked flesh of Michael's buttocks and hit the on switch. A sheet of blinding white pain shot through the boy's body from his shoulders to his toes. An animal-like scream of agony tore from deep within him. His whole body was on fire, his nerves searing from the voltage eating into them! The tortured shrieks ripped through the dark basement, reverberat-ing off the concrete walls and the ceiling timbers. He was past the ability to struggle when he fuzzily realized that the vicious machine had finally been turned off. He was just beginning to get his breath back when another jolt hit him with the force of a sledgehammer. As his mind went fuzzy, his body began to shut down, his screams becoming choked gurgles. He wasn't even sure when it stopped because shock had numbed his mind and his body.

His anger satisfied, Carl released the small form and let it slide to the cold concrete. He replaced the protective rubber shield over the gleaming electrodes of the prod and climbed the stairs without a backward glance. The "prophet of God" was now able to abuse defenseless children without a twinge of conscience. It never occurred to him that he was repeating a cycle of generational anger and violence that had been unbroken for at least three generations. He only knew at some subconscious level that he felt better now, and that was what mattered!

As the summer days grew longer and warmer, the boys began to make more trips back to the lake they had discovered. Carl had scrounged up an old wooden rowboat from somewhere and helped them build a crude pier to launch it from. Since there was no road or even a trail back to the lake, the heavy craft had to be carried approximately a half mile across the fields and through the woods. When finally it was launched, it was worth every bit of effort and sweat they had expended. They rigged crude fishing lines and very soon had a nice batch of sunfish for supper. When they got back to the house, Grandpa Raptors were there, and grandpa, a lifelong avid fisherman, exclaimed approvingly over their catch and then taught them how to clean and fillet them. They all agreed that they were absolutely delicious. The lake became a source of fish meat for the family for as long as they lived on the farm.

A few weeks later, as Randy and Michael were in the backyard, they were startled by a very loud boom! At the same time, they heard a roar from the sky and looked up in amazement to see a jet streaking overhead. It was flying so low the boys thought surely it was going to crash into the trees, but a few seconds later, it had disappeared. These low-flying jets became a common sight the rest of the summer, and they discovered that the loud boom came from the planes flying faster than the speed of sound and breaking the sound barrier, thus creating a sonic boom. They were also informed that the U.S. military was using this area to test their new jet airplanes because the population was sparse, and there would be no complaints about the noise or the sonic booms. It was a sight the boys never tired of, but they had to look quickly when they heard the roar of the plane because they were flying so fast that they flew ahead of the sound they made and sometimes would be gone by the time they heard the roar of their powerful engines.

Several weeks later, they were playing ball in the backyard when they heard the roar of big diesel engines approaching. They stopped and stared in fascination at a convoy of semitrucks approaching in the ever-present cloud of dust. The county had decided to upgrade the road past the farm, and the trucks were hauling bulldozers and wheel loaders and all sorts of other heavy equipment for the task. The convoy moved on past the farm to the blind curve a mile to the west. They would begin where the road made a horseshoe curve around a particularly wet swampy area. It was a spot where cars were constantly missing the curve and plunging into the brushy swamp, nearly always due to the inebriated condition of the drivers. Carl was used to being awakened at all hours of the night by some hapless driver who pleaded with him to come pull his car back up onto the road. It had happened so often that he even had an established fee, usually ten dollars, which was rather a large sum of money. But for someone on foot over twenty miles from town, their options were a bit limited; so the ones who had the money paid, and those who didn't promised to pay. Of course, they almost never did; in fact when they woke the next morning with their heads throbbing from a whopping hangover, most of them didn't even remember driving home, much less getting pulled out of the swamp!

The highway crew began hauling stone and gravel into the swampy area to redirect the road straight through. Grandpa Raptor had discovered that part of his land had gravel underground, and he was selling the gravel to the county for road construction. Business acumen in the Raptor family was basically nonexistent as one could easily discern from their ragtag farming operations, so he was grossly undercompensated for the gravel. The boys found the gravel pit an interesting place to ride horses when they happened to be riding up that way. The bulldozers had sorted out several small boulders and pushed them out to the edge of the road. Someone had carefully painted the words "JESUS SAVES" on the largest of the boulders. The church folks thought this was a real nice testimony to the unsaved community folks until one day someone added the words "Gold Bond Stamps" to the testimony. They were obviously trying to be funny, but the straight-laced Mennonites saw no humor in it whatsoever.

Carl had been scrutinizing his land for signs of potential gravel pits. He found gravel in the woods across the road from the house and with high hopes contacted the county officials who sent some men out to investigate. They dug with shovels, and the gravel was deeper than they could dig, so they dispatched a bulldozer and a huge front-end loader to see how deep the pit would be. Unfortunately, the gravel was only six-feet deep and not worth developing for a gravel pit.

The machinery sat there unused for several days, and one afternoon, Michael went exploring. He had never seen such huge machinery; the tires were much taller than he was. He noticed a valve stem protruding from one enormous wheel and couldn't resist pushing the tiny valve in it to hear the hiss of escaping air. He had done this to tires on the family car and thought these huge tires should really hiss with the valve opened. To his horror, a stream of watery liquid squirted at him when he depressed the valve. He dropped the valve cap and raced back to the house. The rest of the day was spent in fear; he was certain that he had ruined the tire, and his father would be coming for him at any moment to exact retribution. But the day passed and by the time he was in bed for the night, he had begun to breathe easier. He didn't realize that construction equipment filled the tires with fluid instead of air to increase the weight of the machine and add traction.

A couple days later, the equipment had disappeared. It was a relief since he had never been completely sure that his sin wouldn't be discovered and his doom sealed. For many months thereafter, he wondered what had happened to that machine.

FIREBALL AND CHICKEN NECKS

The road rebuilding project crept closer to the Raptor farm every day that summer. The roar of the diesel engines in the huge equipment got louder by the day, and soon, the boys were able to watch the road being built. Where the old road was just some gravel spread on the ground and followed the contours of the ground, the new road was build up so the water would run off into the ditches and the snow would not drift across it so deeply. They installed many shiny galvanized steel culverts to keep the water drained.

One day, the construction boss stopped at the farm and asked Carl if he wanted them to install a cattle pass under the road. He had noticed that cattle were being pastured on both sides of the road and said that the county was offering to install cattle pass culverts under the road for their convenience. Since there was no cost to him, Carl agreed and even he seemed fascinated by the cattle underpass installation. The housing resembled a huge culvert about eight feet high and six feet wide. It was curved on top and the sides, but the bottom was flat so the cattle could walk through under the road to the other side.

It was a great idea—and a total waste of taxpayer money! Trying to force the wild Raptor cattle to walk through that thing to the other side of the road was like trying to capture mercury under your fingertip. They didn't respond well to normal herding, and the sight of that big hole in the wall spooked them half silly. Carl and the boys tried to herd them through on horseback, but they would get about so close, and the tails would go straight up in the air, and they would bolt in every direction, bellowing like angry bulls. It made great sport running them down on horseback, but finally when their milk production dropped from pathetically little to almost nonexistent, Carl instructed them to just chase them over the road like before. It wasn't like there was any danger of them holding up traffic. The road past the farm would host less than three cars on a busy day.

The other wonder ushered in by the new road project was the new fences along the sides. Wherever there had been fences in any condition, they were replaced by new fences. The Raptor boys had never seen fences of this quality before. Not only were the fences straight, the fence posts were all the same size and straight as arrows. Carl had always made fences by going into the swamps and cutting tamarack trees into posts that he dug into the ground and then strung up and stapled to them whatever wire he could scrounge. The resulting fences were crooked, uneven, and ugly; but if the wire was in good condition, the cows would respect it.

Except of course, for Fireball—she would usually hang close to the main cow herd, but was never really happy unless she was outside the fence. She had gotten so wild that at times, they couldn't even get her into the barn for milking. As a result, her udder got so tight from the pressure of the accumulated milk that it developed small splits which leaked dribbles of milk. She would have to be butchered, Carl decreed.

Butchering day came in the fall after the first frosts had killed off many of the flies and insects, and the chilly weather would keep the meat from spoiling as fast as it would in the heat. Grandpa always raised pigs to butcher, and Carl would supply a couple of cows or steers. The dispatching of the animals to be butchered sometimes became an emotional event. Grandpa had a habit of bonding with his pigs. He would give them pet names and spoil, pamper, and pet them until they became such fast friends; and when he approached their pen, they would run to him squealing with delight; and he would pet them and scratch behind their ears. Michael wondered why it was that he could form such loving bonds with his pigs and yet have no workable relationship with his adopted son Rusty.

The pigs from grandpa's farm were put into the corral with Fireball and an unnamed steer in preparation for their execution. Uncle Rusty volunteered to fill the role of executioner, but Carl thought he enjoyed it a bit too much. Fireball was the first victim. Carl placed the rifle close to her forehead and pulled the trigger. The report of the shot echoed off the barn wall as Fireball dropped without a sound. Then began the skinning, gutting, and cleaning. Laddie and grandpa's dog Ring would eat well for the next few days—entrails à la carte!

The adults had set up the meat grinder and sausage stuffer on rough wooden tables in the garage. When the choice cuts of steak had been cut away, the remainder of the meat was stripped from the bones and fed into the meat grinder. Michael always found it fascinating how chunks, strips, and lumps of odd-looking and various colored meat were fed into the small hopper on top of the meat grinder and when the crank was turned would squirt out the perforated screen below like dozens of earthworms, dropping into the dishpan below as smooth, red hamburger.

The sausage stuffer was even more interesting. It was a heavy iron kettle-looking machine that you would fill with the ground sausage and then turn the screw on top, forcing the lid downward that in turn forced the ground sausage out a pipelike tube below. The weird thing about this was that they would select certain pig intestines to strip over the tube, and as the sausage was forced into the tube, it created a long round tube of meat resembling an endless, oversized hotdog.

Back in the barnyard, the boys were examining the remains of the butchered animals. There were the heads, hooves, and skins of the animals, now all bloody and rather gross. Lying off to one side was something that resembled a large overstuffed flour sack. Michael walked over to examine this new curiosity. What he saw both fascinated and repelled him. It was Fireball's udder or "bag" as they called it, and it was still swollen with milk with the teats extended. Michael grabbed a teat and squeezed it. He almost jumped when a stream of milk squirted out. "Hey," he yelled, "you guys come over and look at this!" Even Uncle Rusty joined them as they gathered around the bag and freaked themselves out by milking an invisible cow!

The next week, it was time to butcher chickens. Raising chickens was sort of considered women's projects, and while Charlotte occasionally raised some, Grandma Raptor was much more enthusiastic about it. There was not a lot of "that's yours and this is mine" attitude between the two families. Sharing and working together was a way of life. Chicken butchering created several challenges. First of all, the chickens must be caught. No one would waste a bullet to kill a measly chicken, although Uncle Rusty would surely have done it for sport. The plan was to catch the chickens the night before when they were sleepy and sluggish and stuff them into burlap sacks. Then, they could be pulled from the sacks one at a time to be butchered. Grandpa had devised a way to catch them in the daytime that the boys thought was great fun, but always got the chickens in a squawking, wing-flapping uproar. He had made leg hooks, which were heavy wires about three feet long with a hook formed on the end. The object was to hook their legs just above the feet where the spread of their feet would keep them from slipping out of the hook and then drag the protesting bird in to where you could grab it and stuff it into the bag.

Their method of executing the hapless chickens would have done the crusaders proud. Two large spikes would be pounded into an upended wood stump about an inch apart. The chicken's neck would be stuffed between these spikes and stretched, thus enlarging the target area. The head would keep the neck wedged between the spikes. The executioner would then pull on the legs with one hand to stretch the neck and swing a hatchet or a small axe with the other, separating the bird from his head. It was then necessary to fling the body onto the grass where it would leap, twitch, and flop until all the nerves had stopped to spasm. It was not uncommon to see several headless chickens at once doing the death dance on the lawn.

Then began the cleaning process. The chickens would be dipped into scalding hot water to loosen the feathers; then, everyone was put to work pulling out the hot feathers. When a small pile of naked chickens had built up, the men began cutting them open to strip out the intestines, and the women began the butchering process. Although the death dances could be hilarious, chicken-butchering days were not nearly as interesting as animal butchering days. But the final objective was the same—the Raptors always ate well no matter how poor they were.

*****

As the days got shorter and cooler, they began to make preparations for the rigors of winter. Windows needed to be covered with plastic, boards nailed over wall cracks, winter clothes mended, and a dozen other considerations. For the boys, the most significant change this year would be getting bussed to the big schools. They were about to be carried out of the small community cocoon and thrust into a series of scary and life-changing events.

THE INDIANS

The school bus was coming. The boys stood in the chilly morning air and peered down the road at the yellow speck growing larger by the second. This was about as exciting as life got way out here! None of them had ever seen a school bus on this road; in fact, Michael couldn't remember ever seeing a bus, much less riding on one. This was going to be a real adventure! It was also rather scary. The big bus rattled to a stop in a cloud of dust directly in front of the excited boys. The big double doors emitted a protesting squeal as the driver opened them, revealing three metal steps leading up to the bus floor. Only a handful of the seats were occupied since this route was an extension of the former bus route and therefore the beginning of the student pickup schedule.

Michael glanced at the driver as he climbed the last step and thought he looked a bit scary. He was either full-blood Indian or a half-breed who favored his Indian side. His face was dark and deeply lined, showing obvious signs of years of alcohol abuse. He had no cheery "good morning" for the incoming students or even a smile, just a slightly glassy-eyed stare and slight scowl that appeared to be carved into his hard face. His name was Jake Bordeau, and very little was known about him except that he was the only driver the school board could find who was willing to drive this route. This pickup route was notorious for its wild and virtually unchecked behavior. It would become a dramatic and horizon-extending education for the young missionary boys.

The bus creaked, rattled, jounced, and roared its way to the Indian village of Big Timber, which was the core of the reservation. Some of the stories that had drifted around the neighborhood had always seemed a bit far-fetched, but after a year or two of riding the Bordeau line, the Raptor boys no longer doubted any of them. The bus made one stop at the center of the village where a small crowd of Indian students were gathered. They ranged from a cute little black-eyed girl of six with pigtails to a large brawny man of seventeen named Sam Brown. Sam was one incredibly scary guy in a village full of scary guys. His acts of drunken violence, especially against similarly drunk young Indian women, were legendary. Michael watched mesmerized as Sam made his way down the aisle. Then for an instant, their gazes met, and Michael felt a cold finger of fear touch his heart. Here was a man he would avoid at all costs. Unfortunately, Sam Brown felt just the opposite. There would be conflict! Sam was a bully and bullies thrive on fear, and it wasn't hard to recognize a little scared white boy when he saw one.

The noise volume went through the roof with the Indians on board. Michael heard more cursing and dirty talk on that first bus ride than he had heard in his whole life combined. The guys openly discussed their anatomies and sexual conquests in loud voices across the aisle with the girls who responded in kind. Much of what they were saying went over Randy and Michael's heads, but Carl Jr. under-stood it quite well. Uncle Rusty had his own sex education program going with him.

The new school system was almost as confusing as the bus ride. Michael and Randy were dropped off at the elementary school in Osage, while Carl Jr. rode to the end of the line, which was the Wheatland High School. The Osage school building seemed huge with room after room lining the large dingy hall. They were sepa-rated by grades, and finally, the new school year began. Michael's teacher was an attractive young lady named Miss Jaskens. He liked her immediately because she had a sensitive and caring nature, which served her well with scared little boys, but rather poorly with overly aggressive rowdies.

The day went well as new textbooks were issued and the daily schedule established. The highlight of the day for Michael was a visit to the school library. He stared in delighted wonder at the walls and walls of bookshelves, groaning under the weight of more books than he had known even existed! His gaze scanned the shelves for the Western novels section. He couldn't wait to start reading.

When the closing bell rang, there was a mad scramble for the exits. Outside, the big yellow busses were lined up like a parade, waiting for the returning students. It was not difficult picking out the Big Timber bus. Not only was it the smallest and most tattered, but it sported a permanent blanket of dust from the gravel roads. Michael and Randy decided to take seats in the back to stay out of the way. It took the older Indian students no time at all to furnish them with an education in the error of that plan. The backseats of the bus were the prized locations, much like the backseats of most churches. What little discipline existed on the bus began with the front rows and declined rapidly from the back, petering out somewhere just behind the center row. Had Rosa Parks been riding this bus line, the segregation problem wouldn't even have been noticed.

The party at the rear of the bus became more chaotic by the mile. It culminated in a fight between two Indian girls who wanted the same guy but weren't about to share him. The nasty verbal exchange soon caused the larger of the two girls to explode out of her seat and across the aisle with a yowling screech exactly like what two cats made Michael had seen fighting in the barn. The big girl's fingers clawed for the younger girl's face, but it was no longer there. The younger girl had twisted out of her seat with the agility of a panther and drew first blood, raking her long fingernails like claws across the older girl's cheek. Michael's view was soon blocked by a wall of bodies that had automatically formed in the seats in front of the fight to shield the fighters from the eyes of the bus driver. Jake Bordeau probably wouldn't have intervened anyway, but this gave him the out of having not actually witnessing the fight. The fight raged on until both girls slumped bloodied and exhausted into their seats. Whether there was a winner was not clear, but at least, they had both made their statements.

During supper, Charlotte tried drawing the boys into sharing how their day had gone. Randy as usual was the most forthcoming about his day, but even he didn't mention the bus incident. The boys had learned over years of hard experience not to share things with their parents. Too often, they had shared things that had come back to "bite them in the rear," often literally. Carl's notorious rushes to judgment allowed no time or space for explanations if something came out wrong or sounded bad. It was better to just keep your mouth shut around them.

After chores, Michael saddled Pal and rode out to the pasture where the rest of the horse herd was grazing. Once there, he dismounted and allowed Pal to munch on the dying weeds and grass as he told him about his day. He knew Pal wasn't really listening, but it felt good to talk about it anyway. And he had begun to realize something. In spite of the load of fear he carried, there was a part of him that loved the adventure. He was not a coward by nature, but the circumstances of his life had beaten down his young spirit from birth and, as he would later discover, even before. There was much in life to enjoy, and he would just have to learn to live with the scary stuff!

School the next day was a virtual repeat of the day before. Michael had eaten lunch with several of his classmates who had been discussing Miss Jaskens.

"She's really a pretty good teacher," one of them remarked. "But that dictionary thing is kinda weird!"

"What's the dictionary thing?" Michael asked.

"Oh, you're new here," one of the girls remarked. "If you look, you'll see a big thick dictionary on the corner of her desk. When she gets mad enough, she will throw it on the tile floor, and it sounds like a rifle shot!" Michael could totally not imagine the petite Miss Jaskens acting like that and assumed they were putting him on.

As the weeks went by, his appreciation for her continued to grow. When she had discovered his passion for reading, she had accompanied him to the library to show him how it was organized. He began to study harder than he ever had in an effort to please her. Unfortunately, not all the boys shared his esteem of her. There was one especially rowdy farm boy named Henry, who seemed to delight in being obstinate and disruptive in class. One day, Miss Jaskens was holding a globe and teaching about how the earth was a sphere. She was a bit frustrated, however, in that she couldn't pronounce the "sph" sound and kept saying "spear." She managed to convey the proper pronunciation however, in spite of not being able to actually say it. That was good enough for her students, at least for all of them except Henry, who felt inspired to make some crack about how far could she throw that spear?

This mockery coupled with the frustration she already felt pushed her over the line. In a flash, the globe in her hands had been replaced by the huge dictionary. She raised it above her head with both hands and sent it rocketing to the floor. There was a resounding crash as the dictionary smashed into the tile floor and then total and absolute silence in the room. *The girl had been right*, Michael thought. *It sounded like a rifle shot!* He stared openmouthed at Miss Jaskens who was sweeping the room with her eyes. Her frosty glare settled on a very embarrassed and squirming Henry. Several long and silent moments later, she picked up the globe and resumed her lesson like nothing had ever happened.

When recess time came, the students were careful to step around the dictionary that lay where it had fallen. By the end of recess, it had magically reappeared on the corner of her desk, like a reloaded magazine in a rifle waiting for the next shot.

THANKSGIVING

Thanksgiving Day dawned sunny and cold. This year again, the family was invited to Grandpa and Grandma Raptor's house for Thanksgiving dinner. Although Charlotte was a good cook, Michael secretly thought Grandma Raptor was the best cook in the world. It was a belief he would carry all through his life.

Carl Jr. and Randy were growing rapidly and were as skinny as two beanpoles. Michael was not as thin, due mainly to the fact that he wasn't growing as fast. There were several times in his childhood that he was even a bit chubby, but never to the point of being fat. For some reason, Carl Jr. and Randy started calling him "fatso." In time, Michael began to get upset at this and would become angry and argue with them that he was not fat. This just encouraged them to torment him more, and for the rest of his childhood, they would harass him about being fat. Although he would closely examine himself in the mirror, he just didn't see why they called him fat, but as years went by with no letup, he began to take for granted that he was indeed a fatso. The concept was cemented in his mind by Charlotte and Carl joining into the mockery. When people would comment on how he was not as thin as the older boys, Charlotte would say that she kinda liked having one fat one to prove that she does feed her family adequately.

One night, guests arrived from out of state. The boys hated when visitors came and made a big fuss over them. Without fail, Charlotte would round them up and present them for the guests' inspection and stupid comments. This evening was no different; the guests even wanted to take pictures of them. Michael was painfully aware of the difference in height between himself and Randy who was only eighteen months older. Predictably, one of the visitors remarked, "This one isn't growing as fast as the older boys."

"No," Carl replied. "This one is growing this way!" as he spread his hands wide apart. Michael felt his face burn with embarrassment. He wished that if his father was going to mock him, he would at least call him by his name instead of "this one!"

The self-consciousness about his weight lasted until finally well into his teens, and in a different social culture, it fizzled out. For many years thereafter, he was ashamed of his fat childhood.

Decades later when computers and scanners became available, he spent a week at Charlotte's house scanning old childhood photos. He was about halfway through his first day of the project when a realization hit him like a ton of bricks.

"Mom!" he exclaimed. "I wasn't fat!"

Charlotte looked at him puzzled. "Why do you say that?" she asked.

"You guys told me all my life that I was fat!" he exclaimed. "And I believed it!"

"No," she said. "You weren't fat. You just didn't grow as fast as Carl Jr. and Randy."

Michael was dumbfounded! He had endured a "fat childhood" only do discover he had not even been fat. It was normal for his siblings to call him fat, but rather than nurture and protect his heart and mind from this painful untruth, his parents had joined into the mockery, sealing his psychological fate. He rapidly searched the stack of old photo albums. There were black and white photos, blurry color photos, and photos of everything from fishing to horseback riding to everyday life around home. He had avoided these albums for years and hated every photo of himself and his fat body, only to discover that he had not been a fat child!

Another blight on his existence was Uncle Rusty. He would not know until years later that Grandpa and Grandma struggled with his immoral desires. Aunt Leona was always a little afraid of him and slept with her bedroom door locked at night. When he became old enough to drive, he soon made friends in the community and discovered girls as promiscuous as himself. With his dark good looks, he had no problem feeding his sexual urges, but for some reason, he had to mess with his young nephews as well. He told them of his exploits in graphic detail, including his conquests of married women. Once, he even had to flee naked when the husband caught him and vowed to shoot him if he ever came around again.

He began molesting Carl Jr. first, showing him how to "have fun" with himself and together with him. Michael was aware that something was going on with him and Carl Jr. but never heard much about Uncle Rusty messing with Randy. Randy was not the type to get involved with that type of thing. Many years later, he would discover that even little Johnny had been victimized by this human predator!

This Thanksgiving Day would be Michael's introduction to the nastiness of it all.

When the big Thanksgiving dinner had been eaten and the dishes washed and put away, then Grandpa took Grandma, Carl, and Charlotte for a drive. Aunt Leona was put in charge of the children while they were gone, and she spent most of the time in her room. Carl Jr. had drifted off to sleep, and Randy was absorbed in a book when Uncle Rusty quietly told Michael to join him in the bathroom; he had something to show him. Michael followed him in, wondering why he didn't just show him in his room like he usually did. Uncle Rusty closed the door and told him that he was going to show him something fun. In fact, if Michael was good enough at this game, he would pay him for it. Michael was still confused when Uncle Rusty dropped his pants and underwear. It reminded him of his father stripping him down for a beating, but he knew no one was going to whip Uncle Rusty.

Then, to his utter disgust, Uncle Rusty ordered the young boy to pleasure him.

"*No!*" Michael said. "I'm not gonna do that. That's dirty!"

With a gleam of arousal in his eyes, Uncle Rusty gripped his shoulder like a vise. "Yes, you are gonna do that," he hissed. "Or I'm gonna hurt you bad!"

Michael took one look at the fanatical gleam in the dark, smoldering eyes and knew he was in deep trouble. He tried not to cry as

Uncle Rusty's hand gripped his hair, forcing him to comply. Through the shame and the horror, only one way out occurred to him: *Bite!* He bit! Uncle Rusty howled with pain, and suddenly, Michael's vision blurred as Uncle Rusty's fist smashed into the side of his head. The pain was excruciating, but he felt a little better imagining what Uncle Rusty must be feeling!

Suddenly, the door handle rattled, and Aunt Leona's voice demanded to know what is going on in there!

"Oh nothing," Uncle Rusty replied, his voice pitch just a little too high. "Michael's just being a brat as usual."

He pulled his pants up and strolled out like nothing had happened. Michael washed his hands to put some distance between them and then exited the room. He would never again allow Uncle Rusty to get him alone.

Michael never told anyone about the experience. Not only was he too ashamed and humiliated by his role in it, but also there was no one in his life he could trust except Dode, and he certainly didn't want him to know about the shameful incident.

He was getting more opportunities to hang out with Dode. Often after Sunday morning church, one of them would go home with the other for the afternoon and then return home with his parents after the evening service.

One afternoon, they were riding down a gravel road in the middle of nowhere on Pal and Dusty. Michael had let Dode ride Pal because Dusty had an ornery streak that they were trying to train out of him. One of his bad habits was to make a sharp, unannounced turn into a driveway at a full gallop, sending his unsuspecting rider sailing over his shoulder to the ground. Another bad habit was when his rider would try to spur him into a gallop, he would lurch to a complete stop and stand there unmoving like a stubborn mule until he decided it was time to mosey on.

As Dode and Michael rounded a bend in the road, Michael saw trouble ahead. Five Indian men were walking toward them with beer bottles in their hands. It was obvious to him that they were at least half drunk and were talking loud and boisterously. When the Indians spotted the boys, they fanned out to block the road.

"Dode, we've got a problem," Michael said quietly.

"Actually…," he amended. "I've got a problem!"

"Pal will bust through their line and run them down if they don't move, but I think Dusty will stop for them. Let's get a little closer and then kick our horses into a gallop and try to bust through their line. Don't look back. Just keep riding if Dusty stops, got it?"

"Okay," Dode replied, looking scared. His family lived off the reservation and was not bothered nearly as much by drunk Indians as the Raptor family was.

"On three," Michael murmured. "Let's bust through together!"

At his count of three, both riders rammed their heels into their horses' ribs, and the horses surged forward. The little black and white horse was running flat out with Dode bent low over his neck. He split the line of Indians like a meat cleaver, his hooves throwing stones and dirt clods as he disappeared over the hill.

In spite of his superior speed, Dusty predictably chose this time to be obstinate. In spite of the bruising his ribs were taking from Michael's heels, his gallop slowed to a jerky trot; then, he came to a lurching stop directly in front of the advancing Indians. Michael's heart sank to his toes as the Indians closed in around him and grabbed Dusty's bridle. His usual invincibility on horseback was shattered by a horse that wouldn't run.

"That's a pretty good horse," one of the Indians slurred.

"Yah," Michael replied, despising himself for squeaking like a squirrel as it disappeared into Laddie's mouth. He wondered if they were going to steal him or Dusty or both.

"Is he fast?" another Indian queried.

"He sure is," Michael replied. "You wanna see him run?"

"Yeah, show us," one of them replied.

"Okay," Michael said seeing a gleam of hope for escape. "Let go of his bridle, and I'll show you."

The Indian holding the bridle released him, and Michael made a show of kicking Dusty in the ribs, smacking him with the ends of the bridle reins, and shouting all at the same time. Dusty broke into an unenthused lope, and the crisis was past. When he finally got past being scared spitless, Michael seethed with resentment at the irony of not being able to burst through the line with Dode when he was riding the fastest horse on the farm. Dusty, on the other hand, ambled along without a care in the world.

Dode was waiting for them at Keefer's corner, and they rode home together from there. They needed to put the horses away and get cleaned up for evening church. Michael rather hoped it might be Mrs. Hofenvagan's turn again for children's class.

GLASSES

Michael stared out the living room window at the frigid arctic landscape. Another blizzard had moved in again with an icy vengeance. It had been snowing and blowing for two days already, and the snow was drifted against the buildings partially blocking windows and doors. He was glad for the warm house that protected them from subzero winds outside, but a few days cooped up inside got everyone feeling edgy. Carl busied himself in the basement repairing and oiling harness and tack. It was something he enjoyed doing and usually kept him in a reasonably good humor during these times.

Milking was always an ordeal during blizzards. With the roads drifted shut, the big milk truck that came every two days to exchange their full milk cans for empty ones was not able to get through, and soon Carl was filling every container he could scrounge up with milk. This included a couple of battered trash cans, which he washed out as best he could. The problem with this location was that opening their county road was low priority for the county maintenance crews due to the relatively few people who lived this far out. Since the road had been improved, however, it was much easier to plow, and they tended to get to it more quickly.

Michael had been complaining about his vision. He was constantly reading, sometimes in the semidarkness, and it seemed to be more difficult to make out the words. Carl was resisting getting his eyes checked, which would require spending scarce cash. When at last the storm moved through and the roads were open again, Charlotte made an appointment with an optometrist in Cedar Lake. He put Michael through a series of vision tests and identified problems with his right eye. Charlotte assisted him in picking out a pair of glasses to correct this, which he thought made him look rather good in a scholarly way. Carl, however, was not impressed, and Michael knew his father resented him for wasting good money on something as frivolous as glasses. Knowing his father resented the glasses, Michael tried to stay out of his sight even more than he had before.

It wasn't long until he began to realize just what a nuisance wearing glasses could be. Charlotte was soon reminding him to take them along to school, and Carl was grumbling about wasted money. One evening before supper, Charlotte noticed he was reading without the glasses and instructed him to wear them. When Michael went up to his room, he couldn't find them. He was sure he had had them on the bus on the way home, but they were not to be found. When Carl came in for supper, he was informed of the missing glasses. He fixed his cold glare on Michael.

"Son, get your coat and boots on and get out there and search every inch of the lane and road until you find them," he grated. "Those glasses cost good money, and if I have to buy you another pair, I will drill a hole in your ear and chain them to it!"

Michael could see that his fury was rising and hurriedly grabbed his jacket and boots before his father could become violent.

"Don't even think of trying to come back in until you find them!" Carl shouted as Michael hurried out into the frigid darkness.

Michael was afraid of the dark, but he feared his father much more, so he was relieved to get away without a beating. He walked to the end of the driveway, but it was almost too dark to see, much less try to find anything as small as a pair of reading glasses.

He made his way through the snow back to the house and watched the rest of the family enjoying their supper. He noticed that Randy did not look happy, but the rest were chowing down the steak and mashed potatoes with gusto. It made his mouth water just looking at all that food, but he was careful to stay out of sight as he watched them eat.

An hour passed and then another. It was getting colder, and he realized he didn't have enough clothes on to survive the night. He became more and more frightened as he watched the lights being turned out room by room. Soon, he would not even be able to look in at them and wish he were inside with them. He would be locked out here in the dark where he would slowly freeze to death. He had read that freezing was not a bad way to die because you just go to sleep and don't wake up. He thought briefly about trying to find Pal and huddle next to him, but a trip to the barn in the pitch dark was just too scary. He began to cry silently, the tears freezing on his eyelashes. Why had God made a little boy anyway who was so easy to hate? In the books he read, families were happy and loved and appreciated each other. When fathers needed to spank their children, they would do so sadly and lovingly and then hold the child in their arms and explain why it was necessary to discipline them.

He was sitting huddled against a stump in the backyard when he saw a dark form making its way toward him. After a brief jolt of fear, he discovered it was Randy.

"Mom says you can come in now," he said kindly. "We're going to bed."

A wave of relief washed over Michael as he stumbled numbly toward the door. He wouldn't die tonight after all!

*****

Saturday was firewood-making day. They were going to grandpa's woods to cut wood with him and Uncle Rusty. Carl hitched a team to the big bobsled, and they all piled on for grandpa's farm. When they arrived, Grandpa had his little Allis Chalmers tractor running and hitched to a wagon. The tractor exhaust was sending up a steamy spiral of exhaust in the bitterly cold air. They were soon in the woods, cutting up dead and fallen trees. Carl had a small Homelite chainsaw that never seemed to be sharp in spite of his nearly constant filing on the chain with a dull file. Grandpa used his faithful old razor-sharp Swede saw.

It wasn't long until everyone except Uncle Rusty was hard at work. Grandpa noticed him goofing around instead of working and ordered him to work. Uncle Rusty sassed him off and kept messing around, which led to a typical huge argument between them. Since Uncle Rusty had grown big and strong, Grandpa had become afraid of him and didn't try to whip him anymore. Uncle Rusty had lost what little respect for him that he had ever had, and they were constantly fighting verbally. Grandpa's ace in the hole was the fact that Uncle Rusty still had an occasional bed-wetting accident, of which he was constantly reminding him. Somehow, Uncle Rusty seemed to think that getting married would make him a man with his own home, a concept that he had obviously not thought through clearly. In the middle of their raging shouting match, Uncle Rusty yelled at Grandpa that he was going to "run away and get married!"

"Ha," Grandpa cackled. "You are gonna run away and get married when you still wet the bed!"

Uncle Rusty went stone cold and silent as he advanced on Grandpa with fury in his eyes. He was two strides away and coming fast when Grandpa swung the Swede saw in his hand. Uncle Rusty raised his hands defensively, and the razor-sharp teeth slashed a deep gash across his left palm and wrist. Blood immediately spurted out, staining the white snow with a streak of crimson. By now, Carl had noticed the commotion and hurried over to intervene. He glanced at the gashed hand and ordered Uncle Rusty to go to the house and have Grandma bandage it up and then stay there. He left in a lurching run, clutching the wounded hand with his good hand. In spite of all the violence he had witnessed and experienced in his own home, Michael was horrified by the incident. His father left bruises on the body and the soul, but he rarely drew blood. Somehow, drawing blood seemed more inhumane!

By lunchtime, grandpa's wagon was loaded and the bobsled partially filled with firewood logs. Carl tied the horses to a tree and removed their bridles, while they went for lunch. They took grandpa's tractor and load to the house for processing. After lunch, Grandpa nosed his Allis Chalmers up to the buzz rig and connected them with a large flat leather belt. The buzz rig was just a huge saw blade spinning between two heavy planks. It made a dull scream until a piece of log was fed into it when the noise turned to a twang. The firewood logs were small enough that they didn't need to be split, but were cut in lengths anywhere from six to twelve feet. Two people would carry the small log to the buzz rig and lay it on the planks and then shove it into the huge blade repeatedly, cutting off about eighteen inches each time until the log was gone. Someone would stand on the far side of the rig to hold the severed pieces and throw them onto a pile, ready for the furnace.

Grandma and Charlotte came out to help Grandpa with the buzz rig, while Carl took Uncle Rusty and Carl Jr. to the woods to finish loading the bobsled. Carl had no problem making Uncle Rusty obey. He rarely had to use force on his younger brother, but they both knew he would without hesitation. Michael had once witnessed Carl give him a severe hair-pulling. He thought that was an awfully wimpy way to punish someone, but later, he had overheard Carl saying that someone had told him that that was a good way to inflict pain without leaving marks. When it came to his sons, however, leaving marks was of no concern to him. He would treat his property any way he saw fit!

When grandpa's load had been "buzzed up," he moved the tractor and buzz rig to Carl's farm where they buzzed up the load on the bobsled. By the end of the day, there were a lot of sore backs and hands, but the basements were stocked with ample supplies of firewood, which would last for weeks.

Outside God's Ark

The missionary preacher held his audience spellbound. None of them, especially the children, were used to such eloquent and articulate storytelling. He was telling about how the earth was once so wicked that God wished He wouldn't have even made people; they had just turned out to be a bunch of wicked losers! But then, there was one man who was good and obeyed God. His name was Noah, and God decided to save him and destroy the rest of the savage degenerates. So he had Noah build this huge boat, and when it was done, he filled it with animals and then took his family inside and watched it rain outside for forty days and nights. He had begged some others including his relatives to go in with him. All they had to do was just come in and be safe, but they were having too much wicked fun, and they just made fun of him and his wacky project.

The rain fell, and the ground split open, and water gushed up and covered the whole earth. Every living thing on the whole earth died. But those who had gone into the ark were all alive and well.

"That," he said, "is like the deliverance Jesus will give you if you just accept and receive it." Then he invited people to come "into the ark and be saved."

Michael squirmed in his seat as people went up front to be saved from the wicked world. He really wanted to go up with them, but he was only nine years old and kids that young just weren't taken seriously. But he wanted to get inside that ark so badly! He didn't really know what the whole "being saved" thing was all about, but he knew he didn't want to die outside God's ark with all those wicked people.

When the service was over, he cautiously made his way toward the preacher. He didn't want to get close enough to get noticed; he just wanted to be near him and hear him speak some more. Visiting preachers, and especially missionary preachers, were awesome figures to the young Raptor boys. They were far too shy to actually speak with them, but liked when they could be close to them.

A pang of regret, bordering on jealousy, stabbed through him as he heard the preacher tell one of the men who had responded, "Welcome in the ark my brother!" *Someday*, he vowed, *I'm gonna get in that ark too!* He thought about it all the way home and wished he could ask his mother more about it, but he figured his brothers would make fun of him if he brought it up, so he said nothing.

School life was rapidly expanding his social awareness. He still spent so much time reading library books that his grades suffered, but educational excellence was no big goal in their family, so as long as he passed his classes, poor grades were no big deal. Randy was a diligent scholar, and his report cards were always loaded with A's and B plusses. Michael was pretty sure that Randy was smarter than he was, but all the Raptor boys were seen as intelligent, even little Johnny. He didn't find out much about Carl Jr.'s school life. He had never really bonded at all with him and had a strong feeling that Carl Jr. didn't like him much, which bothered him not at all because the feeling was mutual. It only became a problem when his big brother would get mean and rough with him. Michael had a quick wit and was uninhibited by discretion in making comments and observations, some of which cost him dearly.

*****

Michael was rapidly becoming a superb horseback rider like his older brothers. They often rode the horses bareback, especially in the winter when the horses' warm hairy coats kept their bottoms warm. Carl had showed them how to fashion an Indian war bridle out of a piece of rope or twine string, and the concept really grabbed Michael's overactive imagination. They were simple creations constructed by making a loop and slipping it around the horse's lower jaw and then steering with the tails of the twine. They worked surprisingly well, even on Pal, but it was necessary to keep enough pressure on them to keep the horse from spitting them out.

The Masons had a fat pinto who had been trained to "ground tie," which meant that when her reins were dropped to the ground, she would instantly stop and stand until they were lifted again. In the winter, the boys amused themselves by heading for a huge fluffy snowbank at a full gallop and dropping the reins just before she plowed into it. The pony would set her fat little legs and come to a sliding stop, rocketing her rider over her head into the drift amidst an explosion of snowflakes.

They also tied sleds or toboggans to ropes tied to the saddle horn and had their horses pull them on wild rides around the fields and down the roads. One day, Carl brought home a pair of old snow skis, which languished in the corner of the porch until someone got the bright idea to ski behind a horse. It took a while to get proficient, but in a few weeks, they were skiing like pros. The more they got involved in winter sports, the more winter didn't seem so rough and long like they once had. Over time, Carl and Charlotte managed to outfit them with battered old ice skates as well, which opened another whole world to them. The Mason children, of course, were always a couple steps ahead of them when it came to having cool sporting accessories. Their family always seemed to have more money. So much so, in fact, that one summer, they built a brand new house and tore their old one down.

The Masons also had one marvelous piece of farm equipment—a Farm Hand hydraulic loader on their Farmall tractor. While the Raptors were forking manure from the barn onto stoneboats that were dragged out to the fields and unloaded one forkful at a time, the Masons were loading their mechanical manure spreader with the hi-tech Farm Hand loader and spreading it over the field, behind their tractor.

One winter was so rough that there was almost no opportunity to haul the manure out of the barn where the cows were housed. By spring, the manure was over three feet deep and had been trampled into a hard, unyielding mat. Carl instructed the boys to clean it out, but it was matted and trampled so hard they could hardly tear forkfuls loose to load it on the stoneboats. The stoneboats were crude sleds made by nailing planks across two small logs, which became skids on which the load was dragged across the ground. Their low profile made them nice for loading, but they were clumsy and pulled extremely hard when loaded, especially when there was no snow on the ground.

Forking the hard manure was especially difficult for Michael who didn't have the strength of the bigger boys. After several days of futile pecking, he hit upon the first invention of his young life. He twisted some baler twine together and made a crude rope that he tied to the rafters above where he was working. Then, he tied the other end to the bottom of his fork handle just above the tines. This allowed him to jab the fork into the hard manure and then pry the forkful loose using the string as a fulcrum. When a forkful had been pried loose, it was a simple matter of throwing it on the stoneboat and prying up the next forkful. The idea caught on, and soon, Randy and Carl Jr. were doing it too. But they never gave Michael credit for inventing the system, which irritated him for years!

Several weeks into the project, Carl saw that it was going nowhere fast and made arrangements with the Masons to clean it out with their Farm Hand and manure spreader. It was finished in a couple days, making the boys feel like all their hard work had been a wasted.

BIG YELLOW BUS

The big yellow bus rocketed down the gravel road, swerving and swaying like some insane juggernaut! Driver Jake Bordeau was drunk again. The students weren't sure if he was too drunk to know what he was doing or if he was just in that big a hurry to get home so he could drink himself the rest of the way into oblivion. It was becoming more and more difficult for him to control his drinking, and although there was a nearly continuous litany of saber rattling, his job appeared to be secure since there was simply no one else who was willing to drive that route. The preceding week, some of the older students had discovered a full six-pack of beer bottles under one of the front seats of the bus. Most of the students told their parents little or nothing of the driver's transgressions because there tended to be little or no communication between children and parents about virtually anything.

But now, while the younger children were having a great time riding the jouncing and swaying monster, the older students realized that this was a dangerous situation. Not only was Jake speeding and weaving back and forth between the ditches, but they were blowing stop signs without so much as a glance to check for cross-traffic. A high school boy named Doug commented on the dangerous driving as another ignored stop sign flashed past. There was not a terribly high risk of hitting an oncoming vehicle because there were so few vehicles on the road, but he well knew that it only took one. When the bus stopped at the end of Doug's driveway, he stood at the top of the stairs waiting for Jake to open the doors so he could exit.

Instead of opening the doors, Jake swung around and fixed him with a blurry-eyed glare and slurred, "What you don't know is that on the back side of those stop signs, it says *yield!*"

After castigating him further for his egregious lack of knowledge on the subject of road signs, he finally opened the door and allowed him to pass. A deathly silence gripped the few remaining passengers for the remainder of the route.

The bus rides were a continuing education for the Raptor boys. Little Johnny had started school this year. He was a quiet and sensitive child, and the crazy antics of the other passengers kept him scared silent. The biggest and meanest student was Sam Brown. He was a full-blooded Chippewa Indian like Uncle Rusty, but he was about as homely as Uncle Rusty was handsome. Worse, he had a cruel streak and took great pleasure in harassing little white boys. They had learned to avoid him at all costs, not even looking at him.

One morning, Sam found a new sport. He would grab Michael's arm and twist it hard behind the back of the bus seat until Michael would cry out in pain. Then, he would make Johnny say all kinds of stupid things like "I'm just a dumb white boy" or "I'm a little sissy." Johnny was saying everything he was ordered to and begging him to please stop hurting his brother, but Sam would release his arm just long enough to give them hope and then grab it and start it all over again. This sport and others like it went on intermittently for weeks, and Michael and Johnny tried desperately to avoid him, but they remained his favorite target.

It was a great relief to them when Sam didn't show up on the bus for several days. Then, Michael overheard someone ask one of the Indian girls where Sam was, and she nonchalantly replied, "Oh, he's been in jail for strangling a girl from the village!" He never rode the bus again, and Michael often wondered how rough his treatment of him would have gotten over time?

*****

There was also a new addition to the Raptor family, a fifth and final boy his parents had named Eli. Eli had soft blond hair that formed a curly wave on top of his head from front to back. He was little appreciated by his brothers at meal times when he tended to sit in his high chair and screw his face into something resembling an elderly possum and wail like a tormented gargoyle! Carl seemed remarkably patient with his antics, but his brothers wanted to smack his wailing mouth until he closed it.

*****

Michael was learning how to trade for things at school. His schoolmates were deeply into playing marbles, and marbles were the main currency. When you won a game of marbles, you got to take the marbles from the other players, and they became as valuable as cash, which was in extremely short supply. One of his friends had a shiny silver toy cash register with a real drawer that opened when you pulled the handle. He finally accumulated enough assets to trade for it and brought it home and set it on the battered old dresser in his and Randy's bedroom.

A few weeks later, grandpas came over for the evening, and he was proudly showing them how it worked. He pulled down on the lever and the drawer popped open to reveal his life savings, one dollar bill and some change. He noticed Uncle Rusty seemed real interested in it, and it made him feel good. The good feeling evaporated instantly the next morning, however, when he opened the drawer to find it empty. He felt sick at heart. It took him so long to save even a few cents, and he had accumulated a whole dollar plus some change only to have it stolen. He told Charlotte about the theft, and she discussed it with grandma, but Uncle Rusty of course denied it, and it was impossible to prove that he had taken the money. He was starting to run with a wild group of friends, drinking, smoking, partying, and carousing; and Grandma said that he was stealing from them all the time. Michael had observed him more than once siphoning gas from Grandpa's car to put in his buddies' cars.

He finally landed a job pumping gas at a gas station. He had a likeable personality when he chose to turn it on, and his boss liked him for the job where he interacted with people who came and went.

His boss was, however, getting frustrated with his undependable work ethic. He had been warned several times that he would be fired if he didn't learn to show up for work as scheduled, and the last time his boss had been really steamed, and told him in no uncertain terms that if he skipped work one more time, he was out of a job. One evening shortly after that warning, he was busy pumping gas when a carload of his friends rolled in. As he pumped their battered clunker full of gas, they badgered him to jump in with them and go party. It took every ounce of willpower he possessed to decline, but he really needed the job, and he knew his boss had been serious about firing him next time. He sadly watched them pull away, joking and laughing, smoking, and drinking.

The next time he saw them, he was looking down into their coffins. The sheriff said that he didn't know for sure how fast they were actually going when their car left the road and wrapped around the big tree, but the speedometer was stuck at ninety miles per hour! The carnage was awful, with all five youths dead at the scene, some in pieces. Uncle Rusty's demanding boss had unwittingly saved his life.

He was a sobered and shaken young man for the next few weeks. Not only did he start showing up in church again, but also Michael was amazed to see him crying there several times. Grandma and grandpa's hopes soared that at last, he had come to his senses and would abandon his wild lifestyle. But it didn't take him long to find new friends, and he was soon back to the wild life. He was big, tough, and wild and loved to fight, especially after a few drinks. One evening at the supper table, he announced that a Navy recruiter had been at their school that day, and he planned to sign to serve in the U.S. Navy after graduation. Although the Mennonite religion strictly forbade any form of military service, Grandpa secretly hoped that the Navy would teach him some discipline. But it was not to be. After a short and undistinguished career there, Rusty was dishonorably discharged for constantly fighting with his fellow sailors. Michael wondered how one could get kicked out of a fighting force for fighting too much?

Although Danny Mason did not run with Uncle Rusty's pack of wild friends, they hung out together and did things like fishing and hunting. One day, when Michael's family was at grandpa's, Danny buzzed in on a motor scooter. Carl Jr., Randy, and Michael agreed that it was the most fun thing they had ever done. It was thrilling to watch the ground flash past beneath you from the back of a horse, but there was something even cooler about buzzing along with your feet just a few inches above the ground.

They were also spending more time swimming and fishing. Grandpa was an avid fisherman, and he taught them how to bait their hooks and how to release the flopping fish from the hooks when they were landed inside the boat. He also showed them how to clean and fillet them and how to dispose of the entrails properly so they wouldn't draw varmints like the cute but ever so smelly skunks. It seemed that nearly everyone either lived by a lake or had a lake on their property like the Raptor farm. All it really took was some fishline with a hook on the end and a wriggling worm, and you could catch fish.

There was a lively and interesting young lady named Fern from church who operated a lakeside resort with her mother Ima. They had invited the Raptor family over for Sunday dinner, and afterward, Michael wandered down to the boat docks. He was lying on his stomach peering into the water when he noticed it was teeming with fish. Their religion did not allow fishing on Sunday, so he knew better than to ask Fern for a fishing pole, but he poked around the sheds until he found a length of fishline and a discarded hook. Then, trying to look casual, he wandered into the kitchen in search of something to use for bait. He had to settle for an orange since all the food had been put away and the dishes washed. He began to surreptitiously catch fish and release them again. Randy soon noticed what he was doing and joined him. A while later, the last orange slice had been used, and they had no more bait. They began dangling empty hooks in the water, and to their amazement, the fish kept biting! The fun lasted until Charlotte noticed them profaning "the Lord's Day" and sternly ordered them to cease and desist.

BOOKS, BELTS, AND BEAVERS

Michael stared at the picture in his Social Studies book as a surge of hot anger washed over him. It was a picture of a peasant from an old social caste system being beaten by his master. The peasant was down on his knees with his arms extended, pleading for mercy as his master beat him cruelly with a club. It infuriated Michael that any human being could abuse and demean another like that. Miss Jaskens told him that this kind of cruelty has gone on all over the world for as long as man has existed and would continue to go on until the end of the world.

"The world," she said sadly, "is controlled by the strongest people, just like the forest and jungle is controlled by the strongest animals." He would carry that picture in his mind for the rest of his life.

Michael could not get enough of the wonderful world of books. He especially liked books that had anything to do with horses, like novels about the Wild West. While his efforts toward scholastic excellence were tepid at best, he excelled in English class, where his work was often held up by the teacher as an example for the class. Essays and book reports were his favorite assignments, so much so that they often got rather lengthy. He also had a natural gift for putting words together to write stories or poetry. In eighth grade, he was stunned when his teacher asked if she could publish his latest poem in the local paper. He said that he really didn't want her to, which she had difficulty understanding. She couldn't know that he had learned the hard way in his young life that drawing attention to yourself makes you vulnerable. He just wrote for the pleasure of it, the same as he read for pleasure.

One of Michael's front teeth had a large, unsightly cavity in the front, and one day, his teacher commented that he really needed to get it fixed. That night, he told Charlotte what the teacher had said, and it was decided that his father would pick him up after school and take him to a dentist.

The dentist's office was totally intimidating with all the hustle and bustle, not to mention the vicious-looking tools. The doctor gave him some Novocain and instructed him to hold up his hand if it hurt while he was drilling. He activated the screaming drill and began drilling in the cavity when Michael felt a sharp stab of pain. As instructed, he rather shyly held up his left hand a few inches. The dentist didn't seem to notice and kept right on drilling as the pain kept getting sharper. Michael raised his hand a few inches higher as the pain increased, but still the dentist seemed not to notice. He was getting a bit frantic and began to wave the signaling hand around in front of the dentist's goggles.

He seemed to take a mild interest as he murmured, "Oh, it's surely not hurting much is it?"

He realized that the "raise your hand" thing had just been a distraction, and he would have to live with whatever pain got past the Novocain. The repaired tooth looked so much better that Michael soon forgot the pain of fixing it.

The days were getting longer and warmer as spring arrived. The Raptor boys were eager for school to be out for summer break. The clunky old school bus was getting ever more undependable. Michael didn't mind when it broke down on the way to school, but it really irritated him when it broke down on the way home. Several times on the way to school, it had broken down, and Paul had sent a couple of the older boys to find a phone and call the school. Then, they had had to wait until another bus had unloaded its passengers and came to pick them up. It was rather nice to ride these busses, since they always seemed to be bigger and nicer, and the drivers were friendly and sometimes would even talk and joke with the students.

One very warm afternoon, the old bus clunked out again on the way home. This time, it was in a very remote stretch of road with the nearest house about eight miles away. Paul decided he had better go for help himself, leaving the remaining students with strict orders to stay on the bus. Fortunately, they were past the Indian village, so the wildest of the students were already off, but it wasn't long until things started getting lively. The afternoon sun beating down also made the interior of the bus unbearably hot, and some of the windows would open, and some of them were permanently stuck shut. The windows had an upper pane, which was made to slide down, and a lower pane, which was supposed to slide up. Michael had found a lower pane that he was able to slide up and had stuck his face out through it for some outside air. He was watching the birds in the woods hopping from bush to bush when he suddenly felt something smash into the top of his head. One of the older boys had deliberately grabbed the opened window pane over his head and slammed it down on top of his head. The force of the blow rammed his chin down onto the bottom sash, and pain was shooting from his damaged chin and his cranium at the same time. The older boy stood and laughed at him as he tried to cradle the top and bottom of his head at the same time. He tried not to let the bully see him cry, but it just hurt too much. Hot tears slid down his face, giving the bully something more to make fun of. His world was all about the survival of the fittest, and Michael was just not the fittest! He lived to escape into his library books or on the back of his tough little horse who was very good at the survival game.

Michael was riding Pal one Saturday morning when he heard terrible screams coming out of the house. Both the doors to the porch and from the porch into the kitchen were open, and he had a clear view inside. What he saw would be seared into his visual memory forever! Carl had his oldest son bent over the kitchen table forcing him to grip the edges of the table with his hands. Carl's face was twisted into an insane mask of fury as he swing his heavy leather belt with both hands, pouring his fury into his screaming son. Michael had seen his oldest brother being whipped many times and was usually amazed by how little sound he made. Carl Jr. was very good at enduring pain silently. Today though, he was screaming like he was on fire. Michael watched mesmerized as the big belt hissed through the air, landing on his brother with sharp cracks, over and over again. His mind flashed back to the picture in his Social Studies book, and he felt again that hot wave of resentment. In spite of the cruelty and abuse he had felt and witnessed, he had always chosen to see his father as big, strong, and good. But as he watched his brother being beaten like a dog that morning from the back of his horse, for the first time ever, he began to hate his father. From that day on, his hatred deepened until many years later, he would have to find forgiveness for the man. It would become one of the greatest spiritual struggles of his life!

He often pondered in years to come why that hatred had taken root in him that morning. In time, he came to believe that it was because it was the only time he had witnessed his father's abuse from horseback. He would never be able to prove it, but he was sure that something had passed to him from the proud little horse! He would learn to keep his spirit from being broken when his body was bruised.

Still shaken, he turned Pal toward the road and rode to where the creek crossed. They left the road and headed across Pastor Randy's field to the woods beyond. He rode deep into the woods still following the creek. The underbrush got thicker as he got deeper, until he could no longer pass on horseback. He dismounted and led Pal behind as he fought his way through the dense, tangled brush. He needed to be alone for a while, and he had never been this deep into these woods before.

Suddenly, he heard a sharp "smack" almost like the report of a small caliber rifle, but not quite as loud. It seemed to come from the creek, so he parted the bushes and peered cautiously out. What he saw was absolutely amazing! He was looking at a beaver colony hard at work. The small trees lining the banks had been chewed down, leaving big piles of wood chips around their stumps. The beavers had chewed the trees and bushes down to size and dragged them into the creek to create a dam. Above the dam, the water was pooled wider and deeper, and the surface was dotted with little domes, which were the tops of the beaver huts.

There were no doorways to the huts visible since those were constructed under the water. The engineering and the coordinated work effort were simply astounding! As they worked, they kept two sentries posted on large boulders, one upstream and one downstream.

At the first sign of danger, the sentry would slide into the water and slap his flat tail sharply on the water's surface, creating the smacking sound Michael had heard. Instantly, all the little creatures would disappear under the water. After a while, a sleek little brown head would pop up through the surface, and the sentry would check if all was clear, and the work would resume like nothing had happened.

Michael had read about woodsmen trapping these little critters to sell their furs, but he was glad those days were pretty much past. It just didn't seem right to kill little animals like these who worked so hard and didn't hurt anyone. They never attacked farm animals or bothered people; they just wanted to be left alone to raise their families. He tied Pal to a bush where he could nibble at some greenery and cautiously eased out to sit on a rock and watch the little colony work. It was therapeutic to the turbulence of his thoughts and so very peaceful. He sort of wished he could just live out here with them. But then, he thought, he would never want to live in a world without horses.

DONKEY KING

"Watch out for Donkey King!" Michael wasn't sure where he had first heard that, but it seemed he had heard it all his life. In the course of human existence, there would always be something for little children to fear. Some would fear monsters, some would fear the boogeyman, some space aliens, but to the Raptor boys, Donkey King was all of these rolled into one. He was a dark, squatty Indian who was drunk most of the time and mean all the time. He beat his wife and family with abandon, and existed on government handouts. His shack that he considered a house was located about a mile north of the church building, although Michael had never seen him darken the door of the church for any reason.

Donkey King had made nocturnal visits to the Raptor farm many times, as well as to the other farms in the neighborhood. If the Chippewa nation had ever possessed the stealth Michael had read about in the library books, it had been lost long before Donkey King and his kind evolved. Many were the nights when Michael and Randy would hear the inebriated Indians banging around outside and retreat to the very foot of their bed with all the covers they could find piled over them for protection.

Pastor Randy treated Donkey King kindly when he was home at night and reminding him that Jesus loved him and wanted him to be his child. Donkey King would often settle down and listen, crying and vowing to do better. Of course, by morning with his pounding hangover, he had forgotten he had even seen Pastor Randy the night before and most certainly did not remember any foolish promises to straighten out his life!

Carl had found an enormous iron kettle that he half buried in the hillside in the cow pasture to serve as a watering tank. He had buried a pipe from the pump beside the house to fill it with water for the cows. One night, Donkey King managed to fall into this tank and flop around like a dying fish until he was totally soaked. He finally was able to drag himself out and stagger to the barn where he stood and beat on the door, wailing for his wife "Jenny" to open it and let him in.

"Jenny!" he wailed. "I didn't wet my pants. Some woman poured water on me!"

Finally, Pastor Randy took pity on him and hauled him home, about a six-mile trip. Tonight, Donkey was extra appreciative, and before Pastor Randy could react, he was treated to a very wet Donkey kiss.

*****

With the cow herd thinned out and their poor production, Carl had decided to help Pastor Randy do another mason job in Rango, so he was again gone for a week or two at a time. Carl Jr. and Randy were big enough now to handle most of the chores, and the capable Charlotte always managed to oversee everything on the farm that needed doing. It was by now a relief for the boys to have their father gone so much. But at night when they heard the Indians prowling and banging around outside and in the buildings, they would all have felt better knowing that big strong Carl was in the house with them. Charlotte had learned over the years to bite down her fears and cope. While that helped her become a very competent person, she lost much of the motherly emotional softness toward some of her children. Carl Jr. and Michael felt this the most keenly. Their mother would always be there to take care of them as best she could, but there was a hardness developing in her connection with them emotionally.

Michael had always had a problem talking too much and saying inappropriate things at the wrong time and received many hard slaps across the mouth for his transgressions. His problem was that he didn't take time to analyze what he said or how it would sound before he spoke, and often, it came out wrong. Finally, Charlotte began beating him across the mouth with a rubber spatula. It was painful, but nothing compared to Carl's beatings. However, there was something inside his psyche that got damaged by this, and he would go through life paranoid about getting hit in the face.

It seemed that the natives had been extra restless at night the last while. Charlotte was hearing stories about how wives and children were getting mistreated, and the rattletrap autos full of drunk Indians were becoming a regular sight on the road. Randy and Michael learned to get off the road whether they were walking or riding when the carloads of Indians came by because they invariably would shout at them and harass them. The whites were a definite minority in this community, and the Indians didn't let them forget it. Except for the thievery though, most of the violence was to each other rather than to the whites. There was one sheriff for the entire county, and he really didn't much care what went on. His patrol car with the big round red bubble on top would aimlessly cruise by on the road once every month or two, just so he could say he was doing his job.

Then one night after Charlotte had put the children to bed and turned in herself, she heard the slap-slapping of someone running up the drive toward the house. There was a frantic banging on the front door. She lay in bed debating what to do. They had recently gotten a telephone installed, but there was no one she could think of to call for help who could be there in much less than an hour. The banging become even louder, and she heard a woman sobbing and begging her to please open the door for her! Her heart in her throat, Charlotte unlocked the door and peered out. A sobbing, disheveled Jenny King stood on her doorstep.

"Please," she begged, her breaths coming in long ragged gasps. "Call the police! Donkey's got a gun, and he's gonna kill us all!"

Charlotte's mind raced. This woman had run the whole six miles on foot in her desperation to seek help. Was the alcohol-crazed Donkey King coming even now? Her mind flashed to her little brood upstairs in bed. She *must* protect them!

"Here," she told Jenny. "You call them yourself. I've got to look after my boys!" She raced upstairs calling to them as she ran. "Get up right away!" she said. "We have to leave now!"

Michael was in his first deep sleep when he faintly heard his mother's voice calling him through the fog. He just couldn't rouse himself. Charlotte shook him by the shoulder as she rushed past, grabbing clothes for the others who were now out of bed and fumbling to get dressed.

"Michael is still in bed," Randy said groggily.

Charlotte glanced over her shoulder and said loudly, "Well, we'll just leave him here and let Donkey King have him."

That cleared the fog. Michael was out of bed like a bullet shot from a gun. In spite of the tension, they laughed at how fast he went from comatose to hyperanimation. He was the first one in the car, urging the others to hurry!

Charlotte locked the house, and they took off in a spray of gravel. Since Grandpa Raptor was gone too, she took them to Pastor Oliver's house where they were up late entertaining company. To the boys' delight, they were also eating watermelon, and there was plenty for all. They called the men in Rango, who immediately headed home. Meanwhile, the children began to play a hide-and-seek-type game. Michael was having great fun until he ran with one of the older Mason girls behind a shed where there were trees and bushes to hide in. They were trying to find a good bush to hide in when suddenly from the treetop directly in front of them came a horrible scream, like a woman in terrible agony. They looked up and directly into two malevolent glowing yellow eyes! With screams of their own, they turned and ran for their lives.

When Michael stopped shaking, he wondered if the excitement would ever end that night. Pastor Oliver was not sure what type of wildcat they had seen, but he said that he knew there were some hanging around the farm. Several hours later, Pastor Randy's truck drove in the lane with Grandpa and Carl. Michael begged to go home with grandpas for the night, and since he had had the extra scary experience, he was allowed to go. Spending the night at Grandpa's was a coveted privilege, and Randy and Carl Jr. did not graciously accept the fact that Michael got to go, and they didn't. But Michael felt much safer tucked into the warm bed at grandpas than he would have in his bed at home, and he finally fell into a deep, restful sleep.

When he woke, sunlight was streaming through his window and across his bedspread. He heard the sounds of Grandpa coming in from the barn where he had been doing chores and smelled the delicious breakfast Grandma was cooking. It was Saturday, so there would be no school. He hoped his folks wouldn't come to pick him up until evening.

After breakfast, he wandered down to the barn to see grandpa's horses. Grandpa never had any fun horses like Dusty and Pal; all he had was big clumsy old workhorses, which weren't much fun. He kinda liked the big sorrel mare named Babe though. She was calm and gentle and looked at him with big, sad, liquid brown eyes. Grandpa was not as much of a horse lover as Carl, and therefore, he was much quicker to use his tractor when something needed pulled. That seemed to suit his horses just fine as they stood in their stalls and munched the hay.

Michael strolled down to the lake behind the barn. He had heard the story of how soon after grandpas had bought this farm and moved here, grandma's younger brother Eli had come to visit. He and Carl were only a few years apart in age and had been good friends. They were swimming in the lake with several friends when suddenly they noticed Eli was in trouble. He had walked into an unseen drop-off and was thrashing to try and stay above water. They rushed to help him, but he had disappeared under the water, and they couldn't find him until it was too late. The shock and loss affected Carl deeply, and years later, he would name his youngest son after his uncle and friend who had drowned there that day.

What would it be like to die? Michael wondered. *Would it hurt a lot?* Sometimes he wished he would never have been born. It was just really hard to live being afraid all the time. And now that he thought about it, he was even afraid to die! Someday, he desperately hoped, life would be good, and he wouldn't be afraid any more—maybe when he was all grown up.

DONALD AND QUEEN LIZ

It was Sunday morning, and there was a new family in church. Their names were Pete and Elaine Gleason, and they had a sandy-haired, freckle-faced son named Donald. They were from Nebraska and had bought a summer home on the lake just a few miles from the Raptor farm. They were wealthy, and their son who was just two years younger than Michael was spoiled rotten. He had every nice toy imaginable, but his real pride and joy was a shiny red Huffy bicycle. His parents encouraged the Raptor boys to come over and play with him because he was an only child, and he got lonely for other kids to play with. His parents seemed oblivious to how rude and uncivilized Donald actually was. When it was time for a meal at his house, he would insist on being served first because "It's my house!" When he was at the Raptors for a meal, he insisted that he should go first because "I'm company!"

It was worth putting up with his arrogance and narcissistic behavior, however, for the privilege of riding his bike. The bike became his tool to manipulate the Raptor boys. If something didn't suit him, he would loudly proclaim that if things didn't go his way, he would "put the bike away and all go in the house and sit on chairs." Somehow, between all his narcissistic manipulations, the three oldest Raptor boys all learned to ride bicycle. They immediately began to save money to buy bicycles of their own.

There was a new type of store in town called Holiday. They were trying a radical marketing scheme where gasoline pumps were placed outside a store that sold everything from food to clothes to car parts. If you needed gas for your vehicle, you would pump it yourself instead of waiting for the attendant to pump it for you and wash your windows and check your oil. These stores were the first of a phenomenon that would come to be known as convenience stores. The next time the boys were in the store, they spent a long time checking out the shiny new bikes. It wouldn't be long until Carl Jr. and Randy had accumulated enough money to each buy one of his very own.

To his credit, Carl always tried to help the boys find ways to earn some money in spite of the constant shortage of funds he lived with. Charlotte had a knack for stretching every penny Carl earned and was never a big spender or a needy or demanding wife. Michael often wondered why they were always so poor when all their visiting relatives seemed to have plenty and folks like the Gleasons were downright flush with cash and nice things. He had heard his mother explain that they were there as missionaries to help people find Jesus, but he had to wonder why then did it seem like nobody was finding Him?

There were the special meetings with visiting evangelists where several Indian youths would repent of their sins with sorrow and sobbing and vow to live for Jesus the rest of their lives. They would have kept their promises if their lives had ended within the next day or two; but invariably, in less than a week, they would be seen drinking, cursing, and carousing with the wildest of their friends. Although he grew up hearing about how Jesus healed sick people and changed bad people into good folks, he never actually saw anyone healed or changed from a bad person into a good one. He thought that the infamous Donkey King would be a good place for Jesus to start fixing people, but it just didn't happen.

One morning, an old cow named Queen Liz failed to come in from the pasture with the herd for milking. Carl was concerned because she had been one of the less pathetic milk producers in the heard. He hoped a cougar or a panther hadn't gotten her in the night. After breakfast, Carl instructed everyone to join him as they scoured the pasture, woods, and swamp to try to find her. When the first sweep failed to locate her, they concentrated the second sweep on the swamp. A suspicion was building in Carl that she might have gotten sucked down in the bottomless bog. Several hours later, he located her. She had indeed gotten sucked into the bog, and the more she had struggled, the deeper she had sunk, until all that was visible of her was her head, neck, and back. They returned to the barn for some rescue equipment.

They returned with shovels, a heavy rope, and a tractor. Carl's plan was to dig around her body just behind her front legs and tie the rope around her and drag her to solid ground with the tractor. As he began to dig at the sticky muck, he realized that it would be impossible to dig around her. As soon as he removed a shovel full of the muck, the sticky goo would ooze back into the hole he had made. He tried to shovel faster, but it was no use. He finally tied the rope around her neck and attached the other end to the tractor and ordered Carl Jr. to drive the tractor. As the rope stretched tight, Queen Liz's neck began to stretch as well. Carl dug, shoved, pried, and grunted; but progress was pitifully slow. Ever so slowly however, in barely perceptible increments, the suction of the muck began to yield to the pull of the tractor and Carl's powerful shoveling and shoving from behind. It was late afternoon by the time the exhausted, trembling cow finally reached solid ground. She had survived the ordeal, but the physical toll on her had destroyed her as a milk cow. She was turned into hamburger and very tough steaks on the next butchering day.

The dairying project was by now obviously a bust! Carl was looking for ways to augment his income to survive economically. One such opportunity arrived in the form of his uncle Corbin who had a large and prosperous farm in North Dakota. He was only a few years older than Carl, and they had been close as Carl had grown up in that state. Corbin needed help for a month or two over harvest time, so Carl packed his bags and caught a bus headed northwest. Charlotte and the boys managed the farm quite well in his absence, and a couple of months later, he was back with a pocket full of money and—wonder of wonders—a 1957 Chevy Bel Air coupe in like-new condition. Uncle Cal had bought it for him and would gladly have donated it to him, but both Carl and Charlotte were very touchy about accepting charity. As long as they could work, they would make their own way, and they always managed somehow. They managed to pay the doctor bills when the babies arrived and even scraped up the money to cover two appendectomies. Carl Jr. and Randy had both required appendectomies at the age of nine, draining scarce resources even further.

The new car was the pride and joy of the Raptor boys. They marveled at all the gleaming chrome, the deep sky blue paint, and the unblemished interior upholstery. The clunky old Ford was rarely used anymore, although it still was fairly functional.

One day, former Pastor Wally's wife was headed to town in her sleek, late model Chevrolet. Their driveway was lined on both sides with trees and underbrush. There was so little traffic on these rough gravel back roads that most people pulled out on them with only a casual glance. This was probably why she failed to see the shiny sky blue 57 Chevy driven by Carl Raptor until the moment she felt the tremendous impact and the screech of tortured metal and felt the shower of breaking glass, as the Bel Air plowed into her. Carl had had no time to stop or even slow significantly, but he managed to steer away from her driver's door so that neither of them was seriously injured. Both cars, however, were a total loss!

The Raptor boys were stunned and devastated! For only a few short weeks, they had finally had a car they could be proud of. There was no insurance on the car, so it was sold for scrap. Sunday morning found them once again, roaring and clunking into the churchyard in the tattered old Ford.

Michael felt angry for months afterward at the stupid and careless woman who had taken their car from them! He knew almost nothing about Pastor Wally and his former role in his parents' lives. Carl was not given to gossiping about and criticizing people, but there were many, especially the women in church, who never had a good word to say about him. Where once they had loved and honored him, they now reviled and condemned him for following the path he felt God had led him to follow. He had spent several years holding tent revivals in other states and developed a large and loyal following of very sincere believers. In time, he returned and built a campground with a large worship "tabernacle" in the woods he still owned just up the road from the church house.

Although he and his followers offered repeated overtures of friendship, he was continually rebuffed and condemned by his former followers. It was a hard and painful lesson for him on the fickleness of churchgoers, but he never became angry or retaliatory. Occasionally, they showed religious films in the tabernacle and invited the entire community. The Raptors attended several of these events, and Michael was deeply impressed by the films and their messages. He had known since the night of the meeting when he was nine that he wanted to invite Jesus into his heart when he got an opportunity.

The opportunity came when he was eleven. The church was holding revival meetings again, and the first night he had stayed home sick. Carl Jr. and Randy came home very sober and said that they had accepted Jesus into their hearts that night. The next night, Michael attended the service and followed suit. He didn't really feel an extra strong pull; he had just known for two years that he wanted to do this. At home that night, he headed for the stairway and up to bed. He didn't notice Carl standing around the corner on the register as he passed, but turned when he heard his name. Carl then mumbled something incoherent.

"What?" Michael asked, going a few steps closer to hear him better.

"Glad you went forward," Carl mumbled again, painfully embarrassed to say something so personal to his son!

"Oh," Michael replied, turning and mounting the stairs. He crawled into bed and then lay there thinking about the encounter. It had been so awkward and meaningless to him that he wished his father wouldn't have bothered to say anything at all. Indeed, it had never crossed his mind that he would care one way or another!

A few weeks later, the austere bishop came to baptize them. Michael was the youngest in the baptismal class and was horribly intimidated. The big, bony bishop seemed absolutely incapable of displaying any emotion or sensitivity whatever, and he lined them up and asked them to say why they had responded to the invitation. By the time he got to Michael, he was tongue tied and couldn't manage even a peep of response.

Finally, after a very long and embarrassing silence, he squeaked out, "'Cuz I don't wanna go to hell!"

The dead eyes in the cadaverous face regarded him for several long moments; then, the bishop observed that he was rather young and might want to just wait a while for baptism.

That loosened Michael's tongue, and he said emphatically, "No, I want to be baptized now."

The bishop offered no further objection, and he was baptized with the rest of the respondents in a dry, emotionless ritual.

CHARLOTTE AND THE GO-KART

The three oldest Raptor boys crouched behind a small ridge separating the road from a small gravel pit owned by Pastor Randy.

"This is gonna be the coolest thing you've ever seen!" Carl Jr. promised with barely suppressed excitement. "Last time they blew this pit, there was gravel and rocks flying everywhere!"

Carl was in need of some gravel to repair the driveway, so he and Pastor Randy had visited the hardware store in town and bought several sticks of dynamite. Now, they had drilled a horizontal hole into the vertical wall of gravel and inserted one of the long, round sticks, attaching a length of fuse with which to light it. Michael was as excited as his older brother at being able to witness a show like Carl Jr. had so articulately described. They watched Pastor Randy cut the fuse cord at what he considered a safe distance.

"When they start running, we have to put our heads down flat on the ground and cover our ears," Carl Jr. instructed.

The tension and suspense had reached a fever pitch by the time Carl struck a match to the end of the fuse, and the fizzling flame began its crawl toward the dynamite in the hole. When he was sure the fuse would stay lit, Carl and Pastor Randy collected their tools and began to jog toward the road. Three little heads immediately plopped on the ground with hands tightly covering their ears. Carl Jr. had told them that it would be loud even with their ears covered, and the ground would shake under them.

They waited for the boom. And waited. Several minutes later, they were still holding their ears shut when Carl Jr. began to suspect something was not right. Still holding his ears, he slowly raised his head until he could see over the embankment. The pit was absolutely still. He could see his father and Pastor Randy watching from a safe distance with a perplexed look on their faces.

"It didn't go off," he told his brothers, disappointment clouding his face.

The failure of the dynamite to detonate created a dangerous situation. The men couldn't relight it because of the risk that the fuse had partially functioned, and it would explode in their faces as they worked with it. It would need to be removed before too long though, in case it would be found by children playing or get buried in an avalanche and no one would know where it had gone. There were ways dynamite could be detonated besides lighting a fuse to it. A sharp impact, for example, could set it off. Although there were no laws restricting or governing its use, most of the farmers and construction workers who used it handled it with utmost care and respect.

Michael felt a deep sense of disappointment. It was the only chance he would ever get to watch dynamite explode, and it had fizzled. Even the men looked rather deflated as they all climbed aboard the wagon, and the team clip-clopped their way back to the farm.

*****

"Why don't you boys go back to the lake and catch us some fish for supper?" Charlotte suggested after dinner.

"Sure," they all agreed. "That would be fun!" They gathered their fishing gear and trudged back through the woods to the lake. The boat had been pulled up on shore, so they shoved it into the water by the rickety pier and climbed aboard. Carl Jr. and Randy did most of the rowing. Michael liked rowing, but they usually became impatient with his puny attempts and took over the oars themselves.

They pushed their way through the reeds and out into the open lake, startling some Mallard ducks who had been enjoying a leisurely swim. Then, they heard the haunting cry of a loon, answered by another loon farther across the lake. Michael never got tired of watching loons and listening to their weird cries. Although they looked very similar to the ducks and geese, they were different in several respects. One of the differences that fascinated the boys was their ability to disappear underwater without a trace and much later magically reappear hundreds of yards from where they had gone down.

The biggest difference, however, was the sounds they made. Where the geese made an almost nasal honking noise, the ducks had a distinct quack. The loons, however, made two very distinct noises that were very difficult to describe or emulate. Michael worked for years at perfecting their sounds and eventually got rather good at it. The one sound was similar to a woman getting pushed into a cold lake and shrieking ooh-hoo-hoo, ooh-hoo-hoo, ooh-hoo-hoo! The more complicated sound rose and fell in volume and pitch and sounded also like a woman shrieking oohwoo, hoo, hoo, the volume rising and falling on every syllable. It was easy to see why crazy people were sometimes referred to as "looney." The loon calls fascinated visitors from other states who had never heard them.

When they reached their favorite fishing spot, they dropped the makeshift anchor and began threading the wriggling earthworms on their hooks. In a couple of hours, the bottom of the boat contained a nice assortment of fish in various stages of their final flops. Although they often caught catfish, they always threw them back in the lake. Charlotte didn't like catfish, and there were plenty of the delicious bluegills, sunfish, and crapes to make several good meals.

As they rowed back to shore, Carl Jr. professed again his determination to get a motor for the boat. Motors were very expensive and way out of reach of the Raptor family, but he was determined of get one someday.

After supper and evening chores, the boys retired to the garage to work on the go-kart. They had held a lifelong fascination for go-kart and were determined to build one that actually worked. They had a small Briggs and Stratton engine that actually ran, but were plagued with a chronic shortage of good-quality building materials and an ever more serious shortage of decent tools to work with. Of imagination and creativity, there was however no shortage. They had no hi-tech materials such as steel and welders to work with, so everything had to be constructed with wood and nails except for the parts salvaged from old lawn mowers such as wheels and axels. One prototype after another was enthusiastically wheeled out the garage door for testing on the driveway. They always began the tests at the top of the slight hill leading down to the road to allow gravity to assist the woefully underpowered motor in creating and maintaining forward velocity. Unfortunately, the creaky creations nearly always broke down before they even got up to any meaningful speed. But they kept at their engineering with all the tenacity of Orville and Wilbur Wright. One day, they vowed, they would have a go-kart that worked!

They achieved a measure of success several months and dozens of failures later. Their latest craft had made several successful journeys the full length of the lane. It was time to demonstrate and celebrate their success. They parked the go-kart strategically at the top of the hill and summoned Charlotte from the house to share in their triumph with a maiden journey of her own. When she arrived, Charlotte eyed the sorry-looking creation skeptically, as her sons pleaded with her to take a ride in it. She didn't have the heart to say no, so they helped her climb in, and Randy pulled the starter rope, and the motor roared to life. Since they had no means of installing a clutch, the motor was connected directly to the drive wheels so that when the motor was running, the wheels were turning.

They had two ways to compensate for this—either they start the motor as they were pushing the cart or, if someone heavy was in the cart, they could block up the back wheels, start the motor, and shove it off the blocks for a flying start. It was this method they chose for their mother. As soon as the motor was running, they pushed hard on the back of the machine and kept pushing for as long as they could keep up. It was working! The clunky little go-kart carrying their mother was building speed by the second as she flew down the hill toward the road. Jouncing along inside the crude little machine, Charlotte suddenly realized that they had forgotten to tell her how to stop the machine! She was continuing to build speed, and the junction with the road was coming toward her at an alarming pace as she searched frantically for a means of stopping.

The boys had been totally focused for so long on getting the machine to go that they had never worried about making it stop; they simply stuck their feet out and dragged them on the ground until the motor stalled. This simple plan never occurred to Charlotte; all she could think of was to steer! When she reached the road, she yanked the homemade steering wheel to the right, and the shaky little craft skewed and skidded around the corner and headed down the gravel road in a shower of dust and flying gravel. The boys were ecstatic at the performance of their little machine; Charlotte was praying for deliverance. She could only hope the boys had not put too much gasoline in the tank.

Meanwhile, the Masons had decided to visit the Raptors that afternoon. The drive there had been completely uneventful, until they were almost ready to turn into their lane. What they saw was almost more than they could comprehend! A rickety little contraption on wheels came flying down the lane hill and slewed around the corner, heading directly toward them. Wedged inside the machine was the ever competent Charlotte Raptor, followed in the distance by three ecstatic boys, running flat out to share in her triumph. Despite her predicament, Charlotte managed a wave and a slight smile as she flashed past the car full of gawking Masons.

Mercifully, the motor soon sputtered and died, and the go-kart coasted to a stop. Charlotte emerged unscathed and walked back to the house to greet the visitors as the boys pushed the go-kart back to the garage. She had impressed her young sons for life, not to mention redefining the concept of spending quality time with your children in the eyes of the Mason family!

COCA-COLA AND A BIKE

The thing was after him again! Michael was struggling to flee, but he couldn't run fast enough. As the huge swirling monstrosity overtook him, he felt a searing pain rip through his lower abdomen. Had it stabbed him? He didn't see a knife; in fact, the thing didn't even have arms. He screamed as another white-hot stab of pain shot through him. The pain was becoming continuous, and he came awake writhing and screaming in his bed. Charlotte was soon at his bedside, asking what was wrong. Sweat drenched his face, and he tried to tell her what was happening between spasms. She suspected immediately that he was suffering from an appendicitis attack.

Carl had taken a night job in a railroad yard in Cedar Lake to help pay some bills, so Charlotte called Grandma Raptor who came over to stay the night with the other boys, while Charlotte drove Michael to the Cedar Lake hospital. The doctor diagnosed the pain as appendicitis and said that they would remove the appendix in the morning. He gave Michael some pills to make him comfortable, and they gave him a hospital gown and put him in a bed by the window on the third floor. Charlotte needed to return home so she managed to contact Carl who agreed to come to the hospital from work to be there over the time of the operation.

When everyone had left the room, Michael stared out over the city. The many streetlights and all the neon lights were completely fascinating to him. It was an awesome sight to a country boy from a home that didn't even have a yard light! He strained to see if he could make out the rail yard where his dad was helping move boxcars into formation for trains to carry freight all across the country. He couldn't find the rail yard, but he did see a train running on the railroad tracks, and it was comforting to know that his father was not too far away. The only place away from home he had ever stayed overnight was at Grandpa Raptor's. Everything happening to him tonight was a new experience.

The next day, they wheeled him into surgery and placed him on an operating table. He had no idea what they would be doing to him, but they assured him that it would not be painful. When he was settled, a nurse placed a plastic cup over his mouth, and very soon, he became drowsy. Then, he was swimming in the lake, going down, down, and swatting at the fish swimming alongside him. The next thing he knew, a nurse was gently shaking him, urging him to wake up.

She was all bright and cheerful, saying dumb stuff like, "I'll bet you're glad the operation is over."

He was just so very sleepy and wished they would leave him alone, but gradually, he came fully awake. He didn't feel much pain, but his right side was stiff from the bandage over the incision.

Michael was able to return home a few days later, but he had to be careful to allow the wound heal for the next week or so. He mended quickly and felt so good that it was hard to believe that it had felt so bad at the time. The hardest thing to accept was not being allowed to ride horse until he had plenty of time to heal completely.

Meanwhile, he had finally managed to save up enough money to buy his very own bicycle. He badgered Charlotte constantly to take him to town so he could buy it. The boys were not inclined to ask their father for much of anything because they never knew what would upset his unstable temper and make him turn violent. Carl Jr. was the least afraid of him, partly because of his daring nature, and partly because as the oldest son, he worked close enough with him to understand him at least a little. Most of the time, Carl was nice and could even be fun to be around. Sometimes on a hot day, he would take them all to Keefer's store and buy them each a cold bottle of Coke. A sixteen-ounce bottle of Coke cost five cents if you returned the bottle. On a hot day, it was incredibly satisfying, and Michael made his last as long as he could.

They were all sitting outside the store sipping their drinks and just relaxing for a bit.

"Your dad sure spoils you boys," Charlotte commented with a smile at Carl. Michael sneaked a sideways glance at Charlotte to see if she was indeed serious. He didn't know exactly what it took for parents to spoil their children, but he was pretty sure that it took more than an occasional five-cent bottle of Coke! Like maybe lay off the furious tongue-lashings and beatings for starters!

The day finally arrived when Carl needed to go to Cedar Lake to buy some supplies. He told Michael he could go along to purchase his new bicycle. His excitement was at fever pitch by the time they arrived at the Holiday store. He was out of the car almost before it stopped moving and inside the store. And there it was, sleek and shiny, a deep red color with decals on each side that said Huffy. He wheeled it to the counter and counted out his dollars and coins, which he had been wise enough to keep hidden from Uncle Rusty.

When they arrived home, he discovered that the bike was rather hard to ride on the gravel roads. It was a large heavy bicycle with fat tires and seemed to ride harder than Carl Jr. and Randy's bikes. Michael found it difficult to keep up on the longer rides. But it was still his pride and joy, and he treasured it like his horse.

*****

Life was beginning to change as the boys grew older. For most of their young lives, one year had played out much like the year before it and the year before that. But a growing family was a changing family, and changes usually cost money. The lack of money in the Raptor home was never due to a lack of hard work. There were many contributing factors, not the least of which was Carl's lack of financial management. Accumulating money was not terribly important to him or Charlotte except as was needed to pay bills and expenses. But lately, it had been increasingly difficult to keep up with expenses. Carl was often gone for days or weeks at a time to earn money where there was more opportunity.

Another big change was that Pastor Randy was moving off the farm. One day, Michael heard the sounds of hammering and sawing in the trees beside the garage and investigated to find Pastor Randy hard at work constructing a storage building. Michael was immediately captivated by how he was taking a stack of lumber and turning it into a building and hung around to help as much as he could. He was almost certainly not much help to Pastor Randy, but his quick mind grasped the concept of construction quite well, and he learned much in the several weeks the project lasted. Finally, it was finished, and they both stood back and surveyed it with pride. It was not large, but it was sturdy and covered on top and sides with asphalt roofing material.

Many years later, Michael, who had become a building contractor, would again see the structure, still standing, and marvel at the hideous ugliness of the thing. But today, it was a job well done. Pastor Randy had bought some property about twenty-five miles to the north that had a cabin on it, so he had sold the homemade, child-shocking metal mobile home and stored his extra things in the new building. Although they had been gone much of the time, it still seemed strange not having them around at all.

As the financial stress continued to build, Carl's control of his temper seemed to lessen. Although the boys were bigger and older now, he continued to treat them with a total lack of respect. Michael was usually glad to see him leave to work elsewhere.

One day when he was home, Randy and Michael had gone for a long horseback ride on Dusty and Pal. They didn't get back soon enough to suit Carl, and he had worked himself into quite a fit of anger by the time they returned. They had turned the horses out into the pasture across the road and were walking back to the barn carrying the bridles when they were met by their furious father. He began to shout and berate them. Michael, for once, held his tongue, but Randy made the mistake of trying to reason with his father.

"Don't you talk back to me!" Carl shouted at him. He tore the horse bridle from Randy's grasp and began to beat him with it. Michael stared in horror as the big man beat his skinny son with the bridle. Bridles are made up of large and small pieces of steel, connected by leather straps. The leather straps would only leave welts and bruises, but Michael knew that the pieces of steel could do real and lasting damage. By some miracle, no bones were broken from the beating, but once again, the big man stomped off and left his son writhing and howling in agony. The little seed of hatred within Michael swelled and grew! But he would be careful not to let it show and provide his father with an excuse to work off more anger on him. He had heard them many times tell people that he was such a bad boy that he averaged about one spanking every day. He wondered why parents would ever tell people that about their child. He knew that his mother rarely witnessed the most brutal beatings by Carl, but did they need to convince other people how horrid a person he was by boasting about "spanking" him every day?

Grandma Raptor, however, was unfailingly kind and loving to her grandsons. Michael once heard his mother admitting to a friend of hers from church that Grandma was aware of her son's anger problem and occasionally asked her if he mistreated his sons. Michael knew Charlotte was aware of her husband's brutality, but his mother went through life making herself believe that things were as she wanted them to be. Michael had absolutely no doubt that if his father ever killed one of his sons, his mother would cover for him and call it an accident. He also knew in his heart that if the worst ever happened, it would either be to him or Carl Jr. He realized that he absolutely had to be more careful and as invisible as possible around his father!

THE ASPENS

Carl Raptor was a hard-working man. He was nearly always the first to rise in the morning and the last to retire. If hard work would have been enough, he would not have lived with the constant grind of poverty, which played so hugely into his stress and anger problems. It was also not strictly due to lack of opportunity, although that certainly played a large role. There were a few other families in similar situations, who were reasonably comfortable financially. His biggest problem tended to be his almost complete lack of practical management. As in the case of the cow herd, and the milking parlor disaster, he often used scarce resources to cobble things together that would soon fall apart or attempt money-making projects that would either go down in flames or whimper their way to unfulfilled obscurity.

Such was the case of the pulp-peeling project. He had heard that there was a demand for peeled aspen logs, and since Grandpa Raptor had an abundance of them in the woods on his farm, Carl decided to take several horses and a wagon and utilize his growing crew of boys to harvest some peeled aspen. The trees were not large, making the term "logs" a bit of a misnomer, but what they lacked in stature, they quite made up for in volume.

The project lasted for weeks, with Carl felling the trees with his consistently dull Homelite chainsaw. Randy and Michael each rode a harnessed draft horse, and Carl Jr. would hitch a single horse to a felled tree, which would then be dragged to a cleared area for processing. It was not a difficult job for the horse riders, but on hot days, the sweaty horsehair would grind into their legs, and by evening, they could be quite sore. There were also several other considerations.

One was their need for constant vigilance lest the soft skin of their upper legs get pinched in the constantly moving harness rigging.

There was also the necessity of ducking low-hanging branches as they steered the fast-moving horse. The horses needed to pull singly because there was no way a team could maneuver through the woods without getting tangled in the trees and brush. One horse could pull a small to medium-sized tree fairly easily, but the larger trees were a challenge. They would use the most powerful horse for these trees; and upon his rider's command, he would lean into the load, his big body crouching as his powerful muscles flexed and bulged, his hooves digging deep into the soft earth of the forest floor. Michael enjoyed the feel of the powerful animal under him transferring all his awesome strength to move the heavy tree chained behind him. *This must be how a fly feels*, he often thought, as he compared his puny strength to the big animal's.

It was at these times however when there was the greatest risk of harness breakage. When the horse overcame the initial resistance of getting the tree moving, it would build its speed to a near trot to keep it moving. Occasionally, a protruding limb or even the butt of the tree would catch on another tree or stump, creating a dead stop. When a huge powerful and fast-moving horse came up against an unmovable obstruction, something had to give. That something was nearly always a small strap holding the curved steel bars at the front of the harness to the padded collar to which the entire harness rigging was connected, referred to as the "hame strap."

When a tree snagged and a hame strap snapped, the harness would be stripped off the fast-moving horse like the skin off a rabbit. The hapless rider would find himself dragged over the horse's rump and plopped to the ground in a tangle of sweat-soaked harness leather. There were rarely any serious injuries resulting from their fall, but nearly always some rather painful bruises, scrapes, or pinches. The horse would be reharnessed and the strap repaired, and production would resume.

When the trees were dragged to the clearing, they would be cut up into eight foot lengths and then the peeling began. In the spring of the year when the sap is flowing, the bark of aspen trees is easily separated from the wood trunk. The tools used to peel them ranged from hatchets to tire irons, but the most effective tool was a broken car spring with one end filed sharp. The peeler would wedge the tool under the bark and peel it away in large sections. The naked eight-foot logs were then stacked on piles to be hauled away and sold.

At least that was the plan. But as with most of his other money-making projects, this too came to an inglorious culmination. When the woods was dotted with small piles of peeled aspen logs ready for transport, Carl finally discovered that he would have done well to find a buyer before investing all that labor. There was no buyer interested in the peeled aspen. Aspen, being a soft wood, had almost no value as firewood, so the piles of peeled logs that had taken so much time, effort, and sweat slowly returned to nature.

One afternoon, Carl instructed Michael to drive a team and wagon from the woods back to the farm. In spite of their hard day's work, the horses were always much more motivated heading back to the farm than away from it. The wagon bed was a collection of loose planks laid across the steel skeleton of the wagon frame. For some reason, Carl had never gotten around to fastening the planks down to the frame, and occasionally, they would shift, and he would shove them back in place.

Tonight, the horses seemed extra enthused about the return trip. When Michael, who was standing on the wagon bed, steered them onto the road leading back to the barn, the team immediately broke onto a brisk trot. A trot was all Carl ever allowed them to drive a harnessed horse, so when they tried to break into a gallop, Michael hauled back on the reins with all his strength. Unfortunately, all his strength was not enough to hold the eager team to a trot. Michael's troubles were exacerbated by the shifting planks under his feet. The faster the horses pulled the springless wagon over the washboard ridges of the rough gravel road, the more the planks began to bounce and shift and fall off. The falling planks spooked the horses, giving them extra incentive to increase their speed while at the same time giving Michael less to stand on. He fought the runaway team valiantly as one by one the planks bounced off the bucking wagon to come to rest on the road below. When there were no longer enough remaining planks to stand on, Michael plopped down on his butt, still fighting the running team. The problem with sitting was he was no longer able to see ahead with the horses blocking his view. It didn't really matter anymore though; all he could do was haul back on the reins and hurl invectives at the disobedient equines. There were only a few planks remaining under him when he finally fought the team to a stop beside the barn. He felt like beating the horses within an inch of their lives! He had never really liked draft horses as much as he loved saddle horses anyway. But he unhitched them from the bedless wagon and had them unharnessed by the time Carl arrived with the other team and wagon, loaded with the planks he had picked up, scattered along the road from the woods to the farm.

When the chores were finished, they all washed up and piled into the old Ford to go visit the Masons. Dropping in to visit neighbors and church folks was not at all uncommon, and for the boys, the Masons were their favorite place to visit. The Mason kids always had more and cooler stuff and shared it willingly with their Raptor friends. Also, Carl Jr. was nursing a full-blown crush on Maria, "little miss hottie," the second oldest daughter.

Michael noticed that the coolness between his mother toward Pastor Oliver and his wife had never totally dissipated. He often wondered why this was. He found Mrs. Mason to be very kind and friendly toward him. In fact, she was so kind to him that it made him feel awkward. He was not used to being shown kind, gentle love, and it embarrassed him.

But deep down, he thought Mrs. Mason was one of the kindest and best women he had ever known. He often heard Charlotte and some of the other women discussing and criticizing her when she was not around, and it made him angry. They would pick on the pettiest little things about her and make them into a big deal, and it angered him. He wondered why people couldn't just either accept other people or at least leave them alone.

The children spent the evening playing softball in the large lawn between the house and barn. When it was too dark to play anymore, they trooped into the house for some homemade ice cream. Once again, the Masons were ahead of everyone else with their amazing ice-cream-making machine.

The Masons' most impressive possession however was the shiny red Farmall tractor with its Farm Hand hydraulic loader. Michael had seen Carl try not to look too impressed as Pastor Oliver showed him the machine and demonstrated its lifting capabilities. The loader was an enormously clumsy affair, with the bulky frame wrapping around the front and sides of the tractor. It had a bucket at the front, attached to the lifting boom that had a row of spear-like tines designed to dig into a pile of manure and pick it up. The bucket had a tripping mechanism that could be released by a length of rope running back to the operator. After the bucket was tripped to dump the load in it, the boom needed to be lowered until the bucket dragged on the ground to reset the trip mechanism. It was clumsy and inefficient, but effective.

The tractor also ran with a puttering purr, instead of the loud, uneven popping noise the Raptors' old John Deere put out. But somehow, the Raptor boys knew that their farm would never have anything this impressive. They would always farm with horses and their old John Deere.

TURKEYS AND PAPER BAGS

Hints of modernization were gradually appearing on the Raptor farm. For years, water had been pumped outside, first by a hand pump and then later by a motorized pump jack adaptation where a gasoline motor operated the pump. The water was then carried inside in galvanized buckets for cooking, washing, cleaning, and bathing.

One day, Carl returned from town with their first radio. It was a large sky-blue plastic box with two gold knobs, and Michael thought it was about the coolest thing he had ever seen! Charlotte plugged it in and adjusted the gold knobs until they could clearly hear the announcer on a radio station. Every Saturday morning, the station would have a kids program with a Bible lesson and a dramatized story told by an Aunt Bertha, or "Aunt B" as they referred to her. The Raptor boys would all gather around to hear the stories, and in time, they learned to sing the songs from the program as well.

Most of the other programs didn't interest them, but Aunt Leona and Uncle Rusty who had radios of their own began telling them about stations they should listen to that played "really neat music." The Beatles were getting famous as well as Elvis, Johnny Cash, and others. Michael became very interested in some of their music and had a natural ability to pick up lyrics as well as music, and soon, he was singing along. He was especially taken with a song named *Sweet Pea* sung by an artist named Tommy Roe. Uncle Rusty had seen him perform the song on TV and said he was one cool dude. Michael asked what he looked like, and he said that he had dark hair and parted it on the right side. Michael who had always hair as black as the Indians' decided maybe he would look like Tommy Roe if he parted his hair on the right side too. He tried it Sunday morning and had not quite made it to the car to leave for church when Charlotte spotted the change.

"Michael," she snapped. "You parted your hair on the wrong side. Who are you trying to look like?"

He was mumbling something about wanting to look like his favorite singer, but he saw his father's gaze swing around to take in his new "do," so he scampered back into the house to recomb it.

Michael knew that to be cool like these stars though, one had to be able to play guitar. He talked constantly about saving enough money to buy a guitar and learning to play it, but money had been extra hard to come by the last while and the shiny guitar at the Holiday store cost thirteen dollars and change. It might as well have been thirteen hundred; he simply could not get enough money together to make it happen.

As the long, warm days of summer began to give way to the short crisp days of fall, the financial pressures began to take their toll on Carl and Charlotte. There were school costs and clothes for the boys added to the everyday costs of living, mechanical repairs, etc. One of Charlotte's friends heard about a turkey processing plant in Cedar Lake that was hiring women and men. She decided to put in an application, and the manager must have liked what he saw, because he hired her on the spot.

The following Monday morning, she began working there on the processing line. She was now a working gal. Carl would manage things at home, and she would drive the thirty plus miles each way twice a day.

The job paid well, but the work was physically demanding. Charlotte was no stranger to hard work, but constantly handling the large turkeys day after day plus the long drive there and back each day kept her exhausted most of the time for the first few weeks. As she toughened into the routine though, she began to enjoy interacting with the other ladies at work, and the money she earned greatly eased the financial pressures at home. She had many interesting stories to tell around the supper table about her experiences at work and some of the people she worked with. One of the things that frustrated her the most was the condition of some of the turkeys that got passed right on through the line. Some of them, she claimed, smelled so bad that they burned her nose and made her eyes water.

One day, several meat inspectors showed up to inspect the product and procedures at the plant. When spoiled, vile-smelling turkeys came down the conveyor, the women made a big show of being overcome by the stench in hopes that the inspectors would make the company stop packaging and selling such wretched product, but the inspectors seemed oblivious, which infuriated the workers, especially the women who could easily imagine themselves purchasing a frozen turkey processed by this company only to thaw it and discover it was spoiled! But they didn't dare complain to management. Jobs were scarce, and there were plenty of people out there willing to replace them if they were fired, so they endured the smell and kept packaging turkeys.

The hard life was beginning to take its toll on Charlotte. She had never been the soft, cuddling motherly type, but she had been a model of efficient competency. Never in her life would she fail to minister to her family's physical needs or be too tired to carry out her responsibilities. But life was wearing her down, and she was becoming tougher and harder, physically and emotionally. Women have dreams, and most of those dreams do not include being stuck out on an Indian reservation in the middle of nowhere and struggling year after tedious year to survive economically.

Meanwhile, her people back home were doing well on their prosperous farms and attending their large churches with all the associated social events. She began to consider the options and discuss them with Carl.

*****

The new school year brought several changes. Randy had graduated from the elementary school and was now attending Wheatland High School with Carl Jr. Randy had always been the most diligent student of the four Raptor schoolboys. He applied himself fervently to his studies and was rewarded by an impressive parade of A's on his report card. The Raptor boys were all known as intelligent, especially after the administration of the Iowa Basic Skills (IQ) testing. Michael found the academic studies easy but boring, so he wasted much of his study time reading library books. He knew he had to pass each grade, so he was careful to keep his grades high enough to never be at risk of failing, but he knew he could have done much better.

One day, he was called into the guidance counselor's office for an interview. The guidance counselor questioned him extensively about his life and if anything was troubling him. Michael was not sure what he was trying to get at until he finally produced the paper with his scores from the IQ tests.

"According to these scores," the counselor said. "You are in the top ten percent range of IQs in this school, but your grades certainly do not reflect that!"

Michael gave himself a hard mental kick! He hadn't realized what the purpose of all those tests had been. He had for once in his life found tests that were rather fun, because they covered a broad range of practical things and academic questions. Who cared anyway about protons and neutrons and whether x was greater or lesser than y and z? The main thing he had carried away from health class was the joke about the red and white corpuscle that "loved in vein!" None of the teachers in this school ever tried to make learning interesting or challenged their students to excel, so he rather assumed that it was all about passing your way through the system. It would be his mother's oldest brother (and his hero) who would at the age of sixteen turn him on to the joy of learning and seeking knowledge. Until then, much of what he learned came from things he picked up in the steady parade of library books he read.

Halloween and Christmas that year were both memorable for very different reasons. Most classes in the elementary school had Halloween parties where the students would dress up in masks and then guess who was behind each mask. Spending money on something as frivolous as a Halloween mask was absolutely not an option for Carl, so Charlotte improvised. She had read somewhere that one could make a mask by cutting holes at strategic places in a paper shopping bag and coloring distorted facial features around them so she tried her hand at making one. Despite her good intentions, the end product was crude and garish and looked not in the least like a Halloween spook. But Michael figured that something was better than nothing, and he took it along to school.

The party was held during the last period of the day. Michael felt a deep dread and embarrassment when the teacher instructed them to mix up and don their masks and then guess who was under which mask. *Just what I need*, he thought disgustedly as he opened the bag and draped it over his head. *A paper bag on my head and corduroys on my butt! How un-cool can one person get?* It didn't take long for the class to guess who was under the paper bag!

Christmas was memorable for a very different reason. Charlotte's earnings had enabled her to buy extra nice gifts for her boys this year. The Mennonite religion did not allow frivolous things like Christmas trees and decorations, so gifts were simply put in a corner of the living room until Christmas Eve when they were passed out and opened. When all the gifts had been opened and the ooh's and aah's and obligatory "just what I wanteds" uttered, Charlotte slipped out of the room and came back in carrying the guitar! She handed it to Michael and said, "Merry Christmas," as he stared in amazement. His very own guitar! He spent most of the evening with the instruction book. He had no idea it would be so difficult to learn to play a musical instrument.

Over the next months and years, he would struggle to learn to play it. He tried various "how to" books, but their methods were complicated and frustratingly unhelpful. The guitar was always one of his prized possessions, and he knew he would never give up trying until one day he would play it well. Like the horses, it would play a significant role in the rest of his life!

WURMBLOGGEN TAG

Shortly after Christmas vacation, Pal disappeared from the farm. Michael walked the fence all around the pasture he had been in with the other horses, and although the fence was in disrepair like most of the fences on the farm, he could find no breaks large enough for him to have slipped through. Over the next two weeks, he searched the entire farm carefully and the north pasture and fields, which were about four miles away by road. When he found no trace of the little horse, a conviction began to grow in him that someone had stolen his horse. He couldn't figure out who would steal him, since the white folks were basically honest and the Indians, despite their heritage, had very little use for horses. Besides, it made no sense that they would steal Pal instead of Dusty who was far more tractable and obviously more valuable.

Finally, one evening at the supper table, Carl looked at Michael and said, "I saw your horse today."

"Where?" Michael asked, excitement rising in him.

"I was cutting a load of firewood in the big woods behind grandpas, and I just caught a glimpse of him through the trees," Carl replied. "He was as wild as a deer. I could see his tracks in the snow, but I couldn't get anywhere near him. I think he was attracted to the team of horses I was driving."

"I want to go with you next time," Michael said. "I'll take a bucket of grain to catch him with."

Next time turned out to be Saturday morning. Although it was bitterly cold, they bundled up, and Michael took along a bucket of grain. They drove the team and bobsled deep into the enormous state forest to the place where Carl had seen Pal. There was no sign of him the whole time they were cutting the wood and loading the bobsled. Michael was deeply disappointed, but before they left the woods, Carl rigged a rope in some bushes as a large snare to try to catch him if he passed that way and then scattered the grain in a trail on the ground like Hansel and Gretel's trail of bread crumbs, leading directly into the snare. The snare was unmolested for a week, and Carl finally removed it. He figured the bait had been devoured almost immediately by the forest critters such as rabbits, deer, and coons.

As January turned to February, the weather became especially brutal, with several weeks where the temperatures didn't rise above twenty below zero and several dipped as low as minus forty-five and even minus fifty degrees. At these temperatures, the car tires froze flat on the bottom, and a bucket of water thrown out the barn door would actually freeze on a small pile. The cold and blowing snow made it difficult to care for the horses that were pastured on the north field.

Carl did not concern himself much with the horses who spent the winter on pasture. They could find some shelter from the blizzards deep in the woods where the evergreens would break the sub-zero winds, and they grew long and shaggy coats of hair to keep them warm. They could forage by pawing through the snow to find the grass below, and if the water holes froze over, they could exist by eating snow. This year though, the snow was extra deep, and he knew it was becoming increasingly difficult for the horses to paw that far down to find the grass. He checked on them as often as the weather would allow.

One Saturday morning, Michael accompanied him to check on the herd. To his amazement, there was his little horse, just outside the pasture with the other horses. He was literally skin and bones and so weak he could hardly walk. This pasture was at least eight miles from where he had last been seen, and he had apparently not been able to feed himself in the woods, so he had returned to survive with the other horses, but he had waited almost too long. Carl and Michael set out bales of hay they had brought, and Michael made sure the bigger horses did not push his smaller horse away. When he was in good health, even the biggest and meanest of the horses had learned the hard way not to try to push the scrappy little pinto around. He fought with an awesome ferocity and screamed like a demon as he fought. The few times he had been beaten, he hadn't stopped fighting until long after he had obviously lost the fight.

But now, he was weak, and all the other horses knew it. Carl thought that he was too weak to try to take him back to the farm, so over the next few days, Michael made extra trips to the north pasture to make sure he was getting enough to eat. Within a couple of weeks, he was back to full strength, but although he had apparently learned how to jump the fences, he stayed with the herd. He had learned a hard lesson about running away. His master would soon learn the same lesson in a different way!

It seemed the long winter was wearing on everyone's nerves. Even the teachers at school seemed to be chronically short-tempered and snappy. One of Randy's teachers kept a meter-long measuring stick in his classroom to smack his students with, and Randy and his classmates constantly complained about how enthusiastically he wielded it. He had another teacher named Mr. Joyce that he appreciated much more. Mr. Joyce enjoyed entertaining his students with jokes into which he had obviously invested large blocks of his free time composing. They were always "groaners" by design, usually involving a play on words. Randy's all-time favorite was the one about a little worm named "Motor."

"Motor," Mr. Joyce said, "was a little worm who lived in the garden of a man named John. Motor had a bad habit of finding his way into the house. One time, John was washing his hands in the sink when Motor stuck his little head up out of the drain. He put him back in the garden, but several days later, he was sweeping the floor, and there was Motor hiding under a rug. He returned him to the garden, but a couple of days later, he was washing his dishes, and there was Motor, floating in the water. Growing frustrated, he took him out in the garden again and buried him. Months passed, and he was convinced that he had finally gotten rid of the pesky little worm. And then one day, he plucked several fresh ears of corn from the garden and prepared to eat fresh corn on the cob. He was about to take his first bite when to his amazement out bored Motor!"

Mr. Joyce's students always rewarded him with groans and rolled eyes, encouraging him to go to work creating his next groaner.

Although the Wheatland High School was not short on odd kids, there was one family who was especially despised. Their name was Wurmbloggen, and they were continually dirty and disheveled, much like the Wicksons. The Wurmbloggens, however, were usually covered with scabs from sores that tended to heal slowly due to the perpetually poor hygiene.

The other kids in school grossed each other out with claims of having found scabs from the Wurmbloggen sores floating in their bowls of soup at lunch in the school cafeteria. Ultimately, they invented a game called Wurmbloggen tag where instead of being "it" when you were tagged, you had Wurmbloggen's disease until you tagged someone else and passed it on. These cruel jokes and games were played openly in front of the Wurmbloggen children, although Randy was too sensitive to join in them.

Meanwhile, Michael was beginning to learn the law of the jungle as it applies to humans. It was becoming obvious that people love winners and despise losers. It was also becoming obvious that any form of physical superiority would impress other kids more than academic excellence. Randy was an excellent student, always at or near the top of his class, but he was not really admired by his classmates. There was one boy in Michael's class named Pat who was incredibly intelligent, but he was a serious "pudge." His mother was one of the lady teachers, and she encouraged him to excel, and he obliged. His close friends claimed that besides his studies, he mostly read dictionaries and encyclopedias for enjoyment. Michael thought he must be one sick bugger!

Pat found the schoolwork boringly easy, so they allowed him to skip a grade in elementary school, which put him in Randy's class. Randy respected his intelligence and even competed with him for the best test scores and grades. One evening at the supper table, Randy was sharing about his competition with Pat on test scores.

"He's so smart and overstudied that he can't even think like a normal person," he laughed. "One of the questions on the science test was, what two things does fire produce?"

"Light and heat," Michael replied.

"Yeah, of course," Randy responded. "But he wrote that 'carbon dioxide is formed,' and then he thought and thought and finally wrote, 'I don't remember what the other thing is!'"

The physical superiority was demonstrated by another classmate named Paul. He was a stocky farm boy who started at Osage Elementary the same year as Michael. He had been friendly and common at first, but the football coach had noticed his build and encouraged him to take up football. He did well, and in a couple years' time, he was one of the golden boys, pampered and exemplified by teachers and much in demand by the girls. Michael noticed that the two types of physical superiority kids admired were athletic ability and bold, brute strength, in that order. There were always the school bullies and tough guys that swaggered around the school, pushing weaker students around and taking what they wanted. Several of them like Sam Brown were so big and mean that some of the teachers were even afraid of them.

There were lots of fights that took place outside in the corner where the long and steep flight of stairs led up to the main floor intersected with the brick wall of the school. It created a corner not visible from any of the school windows, and it was the scene of many ferocious fights to determine the order of the sociological "food chain."

It was here that Michael learned one of the first defining lessons of his life. While he was not large or particularly strong, he had tangled with Delwin Wickson on the bus and discovered how easily Delwin could be subdued. Bus fights, however, did not count as status builders. The fight had to be held publicly in "the corner" to build esteem with your peers. Several of the Indian girls began pushing for a match between Michael and Delwin. Neither of them was enthused about it, but finally, the pressure had built until they both agreed. The time was set for last recess, and the word spread through the class.

Michael was not a fighter. He knew a lot about being on the receiving end of brutality, but very little about inflicting it. When he got to "the corner," Delwin was already there. The little crowd of students had picked their contestants and were goading them into action. Michael stared into Delwin's eyes as he removed his jacket. He saw fear and desperation and a bit of hopelessness. They both knew who was going to win this fight! *I don't want to hit this kid!* he thought. A sick feeling was building in the pit of Michael's stomach as he watched Delwin remove several tattered shirts. Michael realized for the first time that Delwin had no jacket and tried to keep warm by dressing in layers of old shirts others had donated to his family.

Then, Delwin raised his skinny arms, his hands clenched into fists. He managed to land a few feeble punches, and then, Michael hit him, just hard enough to knock him down. Delwin got back up and came at Michael again, but his efforts were feeble and ineffective. Michael grabbed him and threw him to the ground and held him there.

"Just give up," he growled softly into Delwin's ear. "Let's get this over with!"

Delwin gave up, and the spectators lauded Michael as the winner. But the faint warmth from their praise was soon smothered by his self-loathing. The thing he had just done was not admirable; it was despicable and disgusting! It was something he would remember for the rest of his life as a display of bad character. He had humiliated a weaker human being for the entertainment of his classmates and to elevate his own status.

THE GETAWAY

As the seasons changed and weeks turned into months, which became years, the seed of anger and hatred toward his father began to eat into Michael's soul. The happy, sensitive child who used to delight in picking flowers to bring to his mother started to become sullen and withdrawn. He was tired of being afraid all the time and tired of trying to avoid and please his angry father. Carl was under ever-increasing financial pressure and relationship problems in the church. He and Charlotte felt that the pastor was leading the church down a path that was too liberal and permissive, and they were determined to cling to the old conservative way of doing religion. There were many conversations and debates about this, and they were becoming ever more rancorous. Charlotte was urging Carl to move the family to Ohio where her people lived.

This option though had a few downsides. One problem was that the church that nearly all of her family attended was conservative to the extreme and fought constantly about such critically important spiritual issues as whether the women should cover their heads with huge black bonnets and cover their legs with dark black stockings. Such worldly things as television and radio were strictly forbidden, and there was pressure on the preachers to force the members to remove the radio antennas from cars and trucks to ensure that the radios were totally disabled. There were other issues as well, and the prospect of moving into this situation was not appealing, so Carl and Charlotte were considering other options.

Meanwhile, the bills and debts had to be paid, and the income was constantly insufficient. Charlotte's job at the turkey plant had ended, and Carl was unable to find steady work that paid well since

Pastor Randy had stopped taking on mason jobs. They decided to try to sell the farm. Charlotte who had more than a fair amount of artistic ability painted a sign on a piece of plywood that read "Place For Sale," which they nailed up on the wooden post holding the mailbox. Although the neighbors were very interested in how much they were asking for the place, no one seriously inquired about buying it. This only increased Carl's tension, leaving him wound tight as a coiled spring, ready to snap.

Michael was thinking more and more about running away from home. He decided that if he ran away, he would take Pal with him so he wouldn't have to walk, and he could get away faster. He would ride down the road, but if he heard a car coming, he would dodge into the trees until it passed. The more he thought about it, the better the idea seemed.

He was raking hay in the back field one day, when he decided the time was right—he would leave today. The problem was that his horse was over at his grandpa's farm, and he would have to walk about five miles to the pasture to get him. But he definitely wanted to take Pal with him. He brought the team of horses to a stop at the edge of the field and tied them to a tree and then set out to get his horse. Now that his mind was made up, he ran more than walked to his grandpa's pasture.

Arriving at grandpa's farm, he needed to sneak into the barn to retrieve his saddle and bridle, and then he skirted the open barnyard and carried them through the surrounding trees to the pasture. A short while later, he was leading his saddled horse through the gate toward freedom.

Pal needed little encouragement and broke into a full gallop before Michael's bottom even hit the saddle. Michael felt a surge of exhilaration as the breeze bathed his face. Free at last! No more tiptoeing around his angry father. *No more beatings!*

A few miles later, and he came to the crossroads at Keefer's Corner. He needed to make a decision. Which way would he go from here? For some unexplainable reason, he had not thought about that detail. Where was he going to go? He pulled his horse off the road and into the trees to think about it. If he was going to run away, he would need a place to go to! Why hadn't this occurred to him before? He had absolutely no idea where to go; he had done all this thinking about how to get away, but given no thought to where he would go! He dismounted and sat under the tree, holding Pal by the reins as he pondered his situation. He couldn't go to anyone they knew; they would just hand him back to his parents. He couldn't just head down the road to nowhere because he had no idea where he would end up. Besides, it would be dark in about five hours, and then, he would have to contend with the night-stalking creatures. He shuddered as he thought about riding down the dark tree-lined road wondering what just might be stalking him.

This running away thing was getting complicated fast! Maybe he'd better abort the mission and plan it a little better for next time. Yes, that seemed to be the sensible thing to do. He remounted and rode back to the hayfield.

The team was standing where he had tied them, lazily swishing flies. He tethered Pal to a tree and resumed raking hay. As he worked through the afternoon, it occurred to him that he would have to come up with an explanation for his father about why Pal was with him. Scenario after scenario was contemplated and then discarded. He finally came up with a plan that just might work.

When the field was raked, he stripped the saddle and bridle off Pal and hid them under some bushes. He would have to come back later and retrieve them. He tied Pal behind the rake for the trip back to the farm. Carl was not around when he pulled the team and rake into the barnyard, but he showed up as Michael was unhitching the team and, of course, wanted to know how Pal got there. Michael had had very little practice at lying, but he knew this had better be one convincing performance if he wanted to have any skin left on his butt!

He looked at his father with a trace of consternation and said, "You know, it is the weirdest thing. He showed up in the field where I was raking today. He must have been out wandering and been drawn to the draft horses, you think?"

Carl stared hard at Michael whose gaze never wavered.

"Must be," he finally grunted as he turned on his heel and walked away. Michael let out a huge sigh of relief. He knew lying was wrong, but he also knew it had saved him a lot of pain today. At this point, the relief outweighed the guilt!

Michael never shared the story of his aborted escape with anyone, even his buddy Dode. He knew Dode would never betray his confidence, but truth to tell, he was rather ashamed of the incident's inglorious ending, so he kept it to himself.

Meanwhile, his adventures with Dode were getting to be more fun all the time. The Mason kids now had a small motorcycle that they rode across the fields at breakneck speeds. One Sunday afternoon, Michael was riding behind Dode across an especially rough field. With all their experience hanging on to the back of wild and half-broke horses, it never crossed either of their minds that this actually could be dangerous. Dode had the little bike's engine screaming and was deliberately aiming for the ruts and knolls that would give them the thrill of being airborne briefly and then thumping back to earth.

It was great fun until Dode lost control on one especially rough stretch, and the two boys ended up flying through the air separately from the little bike. When they came back down, Dode was still gripping the handlebars, but Michael smashed to the ground directly behind the bike, with the sharp edge of the license plate cutting a deep, four-inch-long gash in his stomach. They shut the bike off and examined the wound.

"Let's sneak into your bathroom, and you can tape it up," Michael suggested. "We don't want to get in trouble and have to explain this!"

Dode looked doubtful. His father was a strict disciplinarian, but he was a kind man and his children had no fear of him or his discipline. Dode never had been able to understand the fear the Raptor boys had of their father.

"It looks pretty deep," he commented.

"Yeah, but look, it's not bleeding that bad," Michael replied. "Let's go fix it ourselves."

"Okay," Dode finally agreed.

They headed back to the house where they made a casual trip to the bathroom where the medical supplies were kept. Michael was careful not to let blood drip on his way through the house.

They cleaned the wound and then puzzled over the best way to bandage it. They finally settled on wrapping a white bandage around Michael's entire body several times to pull the gaping edges together and keep it from bleeding. The finished handiwork left Michael feeling rather stiff, but he managed to hide it until bedtime. He was changing into his nightclothes when Charlotte noticed the bandage. It would have, in fact, been hard for her not to notice the white clumsy affair wrapped around her son's tanned torso.

"What is this?" she asked in consternation. Michael explained what had happened, praying she wouldn't tell Carl and make him angry. He never knew if she told him or not, but she left the room and soon returned with salve and a box of Band-Aids. She removed the bandage and recleaned the wound and then used the Band-Aids to pull the edges of the wound together. She continued to keep the wound closed with Band-Aids for several days until it had healed nicely. Michael would carry an impressive scar on his stomach, but it healed well, and in years to come, he overheard his mother several times laughingly tell her friends about his and Dode's clumsy bandaging attempt.

ESCAPED CONVICTS

The warnings were being trumpeted over radio and television. Two convicted murderers had broken out of prison and were armed and *extremely* dangerous. The police had tracked them to the huge state forest behind grandpa's farm where the trail had gone cold. Squads of heavily armed police with trained dogs spent days combing the enormous forest for signs of the men, but they had vanished into the wild timberland without a trace. Finally, the manhunt had to be called off, leaving the neighborhood extremely edgy. It was not uncommon for escapees to disappear into this huge woodland, but until now, they had been mainly thieves and petty criminals. These men were cold-blooded killers, and the authorities warned that they would kill again without the slightest hesitation!

Late one afternoon, Michael was at grandpa's farm to help with chores. Grandma had instructed Uncle Rusty to go out and bring in the cows. He disappeared into the house and reappeared carrying a rifle, loading it as he walked. The pasture bordered the huge forest where the killers were thought to be hiding, and much of the pasture was wooded. Grandma was very displeased about him going out with the rifle, but he refused to go out without it. There was no doubt in anyone's mind that he would shoot to kill if he felt threatened, and the Mennonite religion was very strict on what they called their "doctrine of nonresistance." They based it on the scripture where Jesus commanded his followers not to resist evil, but if someone smacks you on one cheek, turn the other one and let him hit that one too.

Michael had a hard time understanding how a religion could claim to be so nonresistant when they were constantly fighting and bickering and splintering in their churches. He had heard about one young man who had literally turned his other cheek and let an out-of-control guy hit him again, after which he decked him with one mighty punch.

When the church elders rebuked him for his violence, he said, "The Bible says to turn the other cheek and let him hit that one too, but after that, there are no further instructions, so I improvised!" The stuffy church elders did not see any humor in that response, but Michael thought it was hilariously practical!

As the days and weeks passed, no trace was found of the escaped convicts. The police were starting to think that they had moved on to find sanctuary elsewhere. Grandma, however, was not so sure. She was convinced that on several occasions, food had been missing from her pantry. She began to take careful note of what she had on hand and how it was organized. There was much tension in their home. They knew Uncle Rusty had been into some bad stuff and hung out with a very rough crowd. Aunt Leona was careful to keep her bedroom door locked at night for fear of being overpowered and assaulted by her adopted brother.

Grandpa tried to be home at night as much as possible, but he too found it necessary to go to the big towns for work, so there were many nights when he didn't make it home.

One night when he was away, Grandma was awakened by an unusual noise. It sounded to her like the slow squeak of the front door opening. She was sure she had locked it before going to bed, so she lay still and listened quietly. She thought that if it had been an intruder, the family dog would have been barking. She lay in her bed, straining to hear if anything else sounded out of order. She could hear the familiar night sounds drifting in through the screens of the open windows. The crickets were making their nightly chirping chorus, joined by the twittering of the night birds.

Then came the sound of stealthy footsteps across the kitchen floor toward her bedroom. She lay there unable to really believe that there was an intruder in the house. She had probably been straining so hard to hear noises that her mind had begun to play tricks on her. But the icy tendrils of fear were beginning to make their way up her spine! She lay completely silent and still, her eyes fixed on the open doorway to her bedroom. As she stared, the shadowy form of a man filled the doorway. He stood there a few moments, staring at her motionless form in the bed. She lay frozen in fear. The form was too big to be Uncle Rusty and too tall and thin to be Grandpa. It was an intruder! Was it one of the escaped convicts? Her terrified mind raced as she contemplated what to do.

Finally, she decided a bold approach might be her best option. "What do you want?" she asked in a loud, clear voice, free of any fear or emotion. This appeared to rattle the intruder. He stood there a few more uncertain moments and then turned and walked out of the house, making no attempt at stealth. They never knew if it had been an Indian or one of the escaped killers. It was doubtful that it had been an Indian because while they occasionally prowled the barns and outbuildings and stole gas from cars and tractors; they rarely broke into houses. The experience had been very unnerving for them all. They began to contemplate trying to sell their farm and moving off the reservation.

Meanwhile, Grandpa had finally found work that paid fairly well and that would allow him to be home every night. The job was for the county and located in an area about fifteen miles from his farm. He decided to rent a house closer to the project and rent his farm to someone else, thus saving him a lot of driving.

The county was planning to improve another large stretch of county road. The existing road was extremely narrow, and the trees and bushes in the ditches were so thick and overgrown that in many places, it seemed more like a path than a road. The county was look-ing for someone to cut down and remove all the trees back about one hundred feet on both sides of the road. The wood from the trees was to be cut up and stacked, much like the pulp-making project, but without the peeling. Once again, they would drag the trees behind horses, but this time, the logs would be piled much higher by Danny Mason using the Farm Hand loader.

Grandpa planned to use only one horse to skid with, a sorrel mare named Babe. He arranged for Michael to ride her to skid the trees to the landing site. Michael would be staying most nights at grandpa's so they could get earlier starts on the logging project in the morning. By the second week into the project, they had a system in place that was working fairly well.

Uncle Rusty was helping with the project, but the combination of him and his buddy Danny was a constant hassle for Grandpa who was struggling to keep up production. Uncle Rusty had long since lost any semblance of respect for Grandpa and blatantly sassed and mocked him. Danny, as hired help, tried to be more conscientious, but Uncle Rusty's influence was being reflected in his behavior and performance too. Michael was young enough to be impressed with both of them who were big and strong and ever so wise in the ways of the world and sounded so knowledgeable and confident. He began trying to emulate the way they spoke and acted. He didn't realize that although he was a first-rate horseman, he was becoming disrespectful and arrogant toward his grandfather. It was not his grandfather's way to sit him down and point out the error of his ways. Grandpa never really had the courage to do that sort of thing, so except for a few well-deserved rebukes from his grandma, his behavioral slide went unchecked.

They worked long and hard days, and as the weeks passed, the ditches began to clear and the logs piled up on huge stacks. Babe, however, was fading. She was being worked to near exhaustion day after day with no grain to restore her burned energy and very little time to graze. She needed the short nights' reprieve to sleep, but she was expected to do her eating and sleeping and then be ready for another long and hard day. She lost weight rapidly, and her body was riddled with sores where the sweaty harness rubbed raw and bloody patches on her skin.

One evening, they finished up the area where they had been working, and Grandpa ordered them to move to another area farther down the road. Michael was riding Babe with her pulling rigging trailing behind, followed by Danny and Uncle Rusty on the loader tractor. Danny was making a game of trying to run a front tire on the chain dragging in the dust behind Babe, while Michael was try-ing to elude him. It happened in a split-second! The tire ran up on the chain, forcing Babe to an instant stop. The fast-moving tractor kept coming, and before Danny could stop it, one of the sharp steel prongs on the loader rammed deep into Babe's rump. Michael felt the weary horse shudder from the pain, but she stood stoically, while the blood rand down her leg.

It was a bad wound, and Michael was angered by the foolishness that had caused the faithful horse so much needless pain. He hoped Grandpa would finally give her a much-needed rest and bring in another horse to use while she healed. Grandpa however was not sympathetic, and the next morning, he brought some salve to smear on the wound and then harnessed her and put her back to work. She continued to grow thinner to the point of emaciation. When Carl finally saw her after weeks of hard labor, he exploded in anger at Grandpa's treatment of her. But it did no good, and by the time the project was finished, she was a broken and ruined horse, who would never recover her strength and luster. When she was simply too worn out to continue, Grandpa finally gave in to Carl's insistence and replaced her with one of Carl's horses.

Meanwhile, Randy was brought in to replace Michael as horse operator. Michael didn't realize why he had been replaced until weeks later when Randy confided in him that his disrespectful behavior had become more than Grandpa wanted to put up with, so he had replaced him. When he reflected on how he had been talking and acting, Michael was deeply ashamed. He had not noticed it at the time because of the way Danny and Uncle Rusty had been talking and acting, but he knew there was no excuse for his behavior. He only wished his grandpa could have been big enough to at least talk to him about his deteriorating behavior before it had gotten so bad he had to replace him!

ELI

"Where is Eli?" Charlotte asked.

They were almost finished eating supper, and she had gone into the kitchen for a few minutes and when she came back, the high chair was empty. The boys looked at each other with blank expressions on their faces. They had been deep in their own discussion, and none of them had noticed the little tyke slide out of his seat and disappear. Carl was gone for the evening, so he had not been there to observe the Jr. Houdini move either. Randy jumped up from his chair and hurried to the window. He stood at the kitchen window observing for a few long moments and then said, "Yuck, that's gross!"

The rest of the family immediately joined him at the window. Little Eli had toddled outside with his small bowl of food and his spoon where he had found Laddie. He was so small his head was not much higher than the collie's, and he was in the process of sharing his meal with the dog—one spoonful in the dog's drooling mouth and the next in his. He was so intent on his mission that he didn't notice his observers until his mother came hurrying out and brought his benevolence to a screeching halt. Charlotte picked him up, still clutching the dish, and carried him back inside and plopped him back into his high chair. She knew he was too small to understand about germs and hygiene, so she simply ordered him sternly not to share his food with the dog again. Then, she relieved him of the defiled bowl and gave him a clean one with more food, which he happily attacked.

*****

The decision had been made to work toward selling the farm and moving east. There had been no serious potential buyers for the farm, however, and it seemed that they might be forced to hang on here indefinitely. Unless they were able to get the farm sold, they would have no money to pay for the costs of moving and starting again in another area.

Grandpa Raptors were also trying to sell their farm with no success. They had found someone to rent their farm, but predictably, the rent payments were not kept up and the property was showing poor maintenance.

Charlotte was showing remarkable patience amidst the frustrations, especially considering that one of the main options was to move back to her home area and her family. While she was not one to mouth lofty ecclesiastical maxims and clichés, she had a deep, constant faith that sustained her through all the difficult situations in life. It was always to her that the boys took their problems and triumphs. Carl Jr. was the only one of the boys who understood his father at all. Occasionally, Carl would share a small bit of confidence with his oldest son who was able to get brief glimpses into his soul. But they were never able to get close because of the master and servant status quo that was Carl's relationship with his sons. Carl was just not able to admit that he was ever wrong, even when it became obvious that he was.

One evening when Michael got home from school, his mother called him to the kitchen. She had gotten a report that he had called a boy on the bus bad names. Michael told her that he had no memory of the incident she was describing, but she was convinced that it had happened just the way it had been told to her. Hard as he tried to think, Michael could not remember any altercation at all with the boy, and he stoutly maintained his innocence. Charlotte would not let it go; she was convinced that he was lying. She interrogated him fiercely for about fifteen minutes, but he would not admit to what he had not done.

Finally, Carl entered the room and joined the interrogation, and Michael knew that it no longer mattered if he was guilty or not; he would get a whipping. The last thing he wanted to do was get his father angry, so he immediately lied and said that he had done it. It turned out to be a wise move because the resulting spanking was administered by his mother who could warm the behind admirably, but didn't make them strip and simply didn't have the power to deliver the bruising blows her husband did.

When the truth came out later that he had been innocent, Charlotte just said, "Oh well, that spanking can just count for something you did that we didn't find out about!" That logic really fried Michael. He wondered why it was that boys have to answer and pay for every little mistake they made but their parents never have to admit to the things they do wrong? He had, like most children, a strong sense of what is fair and what is not. Many years and many hard experiences later, he would come to understand two huge truths that would greatly clarify life in the real world.

The first truth is that life is simply not fair and never will be!

The second truth is closely related—that whether you are genuinely guilty or innocent is irrelevant. If enough people believe it, you will pay the price. And future exoneration will never compensate for the price you paid.

There is a certain refuge in cynicism, and it began to grow in him before he reached his teens. It was continually reinforced by such incidents as the broken tractor hitch.

One day, Carl instructed Carl Jr. to hitch the small tractor to the disk and get it ready to work some ground. Somewhere in the process, Carl Jr. turned too short and snapped the hitch in two.

The blunder infuriated his father, and he snarled, "This hitch is gonna cost thirty-five dollars to replace, and you are gonna pay the bill, no matter how long it takes you!"

Carl Jr. wisely didn't respond, and Michael thought that he was probably glad to get off without a beating. At least, he surely would have rather paid money than get a whipping.

A day or two later, Carl took the hitch off and took it to a neighbor who had a welder. The man welded it up nicely and charged him seventy-five cents. Carl Jr. hoped that this meant that his bill would be reduced by about thirty-four dollars and twenty-five cents, but it was not to be! Dollar by dollar, his father made him pay the entire thirty-five dollars, a price he had just made up out of thin air!

One of the things the boys always enjoyed was the story time each night before they went to bed. Carl would participate sometimes when he was home, but mostly, it was Charlotte who faithfully read from the Bible and then from a storybook, after which they would have a prayer. The Raptor boys all loved stories and were themselves voracious readers. It was one consistently bright spot in their often stormy world.

One night at story time, Charlotte had put little Eli in his crib. The crib was in his parents' bedroom, which was just around the corner from the living room where the story time was taking place. Eli began to cry, and Michael was sure that he was scared, alone in the semidark bedroom. Carl went in and gave him a swat and ordered him to be quiet. He was quiet for a few minutes, and then he toddled out to Charlotte. Carl intercepted him, scooped him up, and hauled him back to his crib, administering several swats on the way. He stood over him until he stopped crying and then returned to the living room. Soon, Eli began crying again, and Michael could see that his father was getting angry. By now, the tension in the room was thick enough to slice. The crying was obviously that of a scared child, and Michael could surely relate to that feeling! They heard the squeak of the crib as Eli climbed out and again toddled toward his mother. His chubby little arms were raised imploringly as he stumbled toward her, fear and desperation in his eyes. He never made it across the fifteen feet separating them. Carl scooped up his small son and hauled him off to the bedroom again where he gave him a spanking and plopped him back into the crib.

Charlotte continued reading, but by now, no one was really listening. They were hoping that little Eli would stay quiet and in his bed. But it was not to be! He began sobbing and again crawled out of the crib and toddled toward his mother as fast as his little legs would carry him. His face was a mask of fear and confusion! Carl was on his feet, his face dark with anger that his commands had been disobeyed again. He grabbed the child roughly and half carried and half dragged him back into the bedroom!

Michael cringed as he heard the agonized screams of his terrified baby brother over the sounds of the blows. It went on and on until he wondered if his father had totally snapped this time! Then, he heard his mother say sternly, "Randy, stop laughing!"

Michael stole a glance at Randy who choked out, "I'm not laughing," and saw that he was trying to cover his face with his hands. Then, he saw what his mother was not close enough to see— there were tears running down between Randy's fingers and across his hands. No, neither he nor anyone else in this room was finding the breaking of a little two-year-old boy amusing!

After months of trying to sell the farm with no success, someone suggested to Carl that he try listing it with a realtor. He pursued that idea and ultimately listed it with a realty that covered their area. It turned out to be one of the best moves he had ever made in his entire farming career. The realty had a much broader base of interested buyers and began showing the property. It began to look like a sale was imminent! It was time to think about moving. But before they could move out of state, they would need to have an auction, and it was looking like they might need to move before that could be arranged. But the proceeds from the farm would easily offset any inconvenience in arranging the schedule. There was much cause for optimism.

Carl and Charlotte made a couple of scouting trips to Ohio to try to decide where to relocate. It would feel good to finally have some money after all the years of hard slogging.

*****

Then one day, the farm was sold! The deal was made and finalized in less time than they needed to move out. When Grandma Raptor heard the news, she instructed Grandpa to move the deadbeat renters off their farm so Carl and his family could live there while they found property in Ohio and prepared for their final auction sale. The eight thousand dollars from the sale of the farm was put into a bank account to be used only for the purchase of another property. The sorry farming operation would continue over one more winter, and the auction was to be held in the spring.

While it seemed that Carl's stress level would have dropped with money in the bank, the reality was just the opposite. It was that fall and winter that he would commit some of the most violent retributions his sons would ever witness!

Michael never heard the details of what happened to his oldest brother the day his father permanently damaged his brother's back. They had been moving machinery from their farm to grandpa's when Carl Jr. did something to send his father over the edge. The resulting beating left his oldest son seeking chiropractic relief until years after he had his own wife and family. Although Michael and Carl Jr. received the worst of their father's treatment, they never talked about it. As far as Michael knew, none of the boys discussed it. He never really knew if they avoided the subject out of shame or fear, but in years to come, his older brothers would attempt to deny or at least downplay those long, hard thirteen years.

The fall and early winter found them extremely busy between school and church functions and moving off the farm so the new owners could take possession. They never participated in any school functions, but were very faithful in supporting the church and its related activities. Michael and Randy discussed the odd coolness between their parents and Pastor Mason and his wife several times. Except for the way they had heard their mother join in with other women who talked bad about Mrs. Mason behind her back, they never witnessed any overt hostility between them, but it was odd, especially the way they tried to keep space between Carl Jr. and the lively little Miss Maria.

By the time winter had set in, the ancient machinery had all been moved to Grandpa's farm and the cows were settled in their stanchions in the barn. Grandpa's barn was more modern than Carl's. He had two rows of stanchions, which were two vertical metal bars approximately four feet long that would spread at the top to allow the cow to insert her head to reach the manger on the other side. Then, the bars would be closed and locked together about eight inches apart, allowing a fair amount of head movement but trapping the head from coming back out. Milking the cows in this system was much more organized than the pitiful wooden "milking parlor."

There were also several tie stalls for the more fortunate horses. These were, of course, the workhorses. Carl loved the saddle horses, but it seemed that his very favorites were always the draft horses. Every horse on the farm had to be able to work under harness if called upon. But Randy and Michael's horses were not very valuable as pulling machines. Dusty was mostly quarter horse, the breed tremendously popular for working cattle and performing in rodeo events. Under a saddle, he was all class and spirit and speed. But under a harness, he became a dopey, unmotivated creature, plodding along like an automaton.

Pal continued to be the real piece of work. He had perfected his trace-busting routine to the point where Carl rarely harnessed him anymore. But Michael had witnessed a few performances where his little horse had settled down and dug in and actually outpulled the much larger draft horse hitched beside him. Those occasions were rare, however, and not worth Carl's time to repair his multiple harness breaks.

One Sunday evening in midwinter, the scene in the house was chaotic. Chores had taken extralong, and everyone was scrambling to get ready for church. Everyone was uptight except little Johnny who seemed to be doing his best to get on his brothers' nerves. He had several little sayings that he used over and over until his older brothers wanted to strangle him! Some his brothers found rather amusing, like the way he would mimic the austere old bishop saying, "Testimonies. Testimonies?" Others got really irritating, like saying, "Zzzzzzzzzzz," when someone got upset, or "Pull the pennies outa your pig," when someone needed something. There were also a few multipurpose aphorisms like, "Apples and pears, who cares."

Michael was standing on the large register outside his parents' bedroom tying his shoes when his shoelace broke for about the third time. "Mom," he called. "I need some new shoelaces."

"Pull the pennies outa your pig!" Johnny advised from the kitchen.

"Just don't you worry about the pennies in my pig!" Michael snapped.

"Michael," Charlotte chided. "Don't talk mean."

"Well, he started it," Michael said, still trying to splice the remaining length of shoelace.

Without warning, Carl exploded from their bedroom. He grabbed Michael by the hair and rammed his neck into the crook of his left elbow; then, his arm closed on it like a vise. It happened so fast and so out of the blue that his powerful fist was smashing into Michael's face for the third time before he even realized that he was in trouble. Although he was now thirteen years old, he was small for his age and not terribly strong. His writhing to escape the headlock was totally ineffective in the grip of such a powerful man, and his face was taking a terrible pounding. This was a very different kind of pain than he was used to—less sharp but deep and harsh. He felt the tissue of his face being crushed, felt the knuckles grind into his cheekbones with every blow! His usual fear was slightly offset by the speed of the attack and his bewilderment over what had caused it and the unusual nature of the beating. When Carl's rage had cooled, he thrust his son away from him like something unclean and strode back into his bedroom. The house was absolutely silent except for the sobbing gasps of pain from the "disciplined" boy. Then, there were the sounds of its occupants exiting silently for the drive to church. Michael walked to the car, badly shaken. His face was on fire and throbbing, and his brain rather fuzzy. *What had just happened? Why had it happened? Would this stuff never end?* his tortured mind screamed. They all piled silently into the car and drove to church to hear about the love of Jesus.

The entire household seemed subdued the next morning. Michael performed his chores and got ready for school without a word to anyone. The pain in his face had settled to a dull ache, and he didn't even look into a mirror as he washed up for school. For some reason, he was fighting a deep sense of shame about what had happened. He really wished he would know what had precipitated it. Had his father thought he was sassing his mother? Did he feel like Michael was just a rotten kid? Or had he just needed an outlet to vent his volcanic anger? It made no sense, but he certainly wouldn't be asking his father for an explanation!

As the school day progressed, the other students began to give him odd looks. He didn't think much about it until finally, toward the end of the day, one of the lady teachers asked him to stop by her room after the other students had left. When he entered the room, she closed the door behind him. He wasn't sure what this might be about, but he suspected it would be another lecture on why he wasn't trying harder to get better grades.

To his surprise, there was sympathy in her eyes, and she asked in a gentle voice, "What happened to your face?"

"My face?" he stammered, caught completely off guard. "What do you mean?"

"I think you know what I mean," she said quietly. "Your face is all purple. Did someone hurt you?"

Michael's mind raced. He had not looked at his face since the beating and was caught completely off guard. But he was becoming an accomplished liar and rose to the occasion. "Oh that," he said with an attempted casualness that sounded fake even to him. "I took a hard fall last night while I was doing chores."

"Will you tell me about it?" she asked.

"Well, it's kinda embarrassing," he responded, his mind racing to create a cover story.

By the time his tale was complete, he was rather impressed with it himself, but he could see the teacher was less than convinced. He felt bad about lying to her, like he felt bad every time he lied. He knew very well what the Bible says about lying; but to him, it was a tool, one of the very few he had, of survival. He would have to sort it out with God sometime in the future.

When she dismissed him, he went directly to the bathroom to examine his reflection. He was shocked by the mottled purple and green face that stared back from the mirror. It was no wonder that he had been getting odd looks from his classmates that day! His father had set a new benchmark. The bruises on his face would heal completely. But the feel of his father's knuckles grinding into his cheekbones would remain clearly etched in his memory until his dying day!

THE AUCTION

Auction sale day was approaching fast. The sale bills had been printed and circulated. Farmers from quite a distance were coming by at chore time to check out the cows and see how much milk they produced. The farm machinery had been lined up in rows in the barnyard, and the contents of the sheds emptied and organized on hay wagons. Even the horses had to be sold. There were only two exceptions, Carl's favorite draft horse, and Dusty, who would be hauled to the new home on the back of the Dodge pickup Carl had purchased.

Pal had been sold privately. Michael had mixed feelings about selling his little horse. He would miss him, but Pal had become progressively harder to manage, and riding him had become more rodeo performance than pleasure. Michael had been breaking a colt out of a batch of six horses that Carl was boarding for a neighbor. She was a well-proportioned sorrel filly he had named Babe; she had a far more workable nature than Pal. He had bonded with her and would miss her when she returned to her owner's farm.

But there was excitement in the air with the school year nearing the end and the upcoming sale and move. Carl had failed to find a suitable farm to purchase, so he had rented a huge clapboard house with a shed and large field where he could pasture the remaining two horses.

Carl had splurged on the purchase of the half-ton Dodge pickup for several reasons. One was that he wanted a dependable pickup for the move, and the other was that he and Charlotte were planning a long family trip to Alaska with it, immediately after the move. They would put a top on the bed and take a tent for the boys to sleep in on the way.

A few weeks before the sale, a final incident occurred. It was a Sunday morning, and things had gone very poorly in the barn. Randy and Michael were already in the house cleaning up from chores, and Carl Jr. came in a bit later. He was not in a good mood and soon got into an altercation with his mother. He was now a strong, strapping young man of sixteen and was getting increasingly resentful of his mother's corrective swats and mouth slaps. Michael had even seen him grab and hold Charlotte's arm a time or two when she tried to swat him. He knew his big brother was playing with fire, but he stayed out of it.

He didn't actually see what started the incident in the kitchen between his mother and Carl Jr., but he entered the kitchen just in time to see his mother shove her son down the cellar stairs and slam the door shut. Then, she opened the outside door and shouted to Carl who was coming up the walkway.

"Come in here and deal with your son!" Charlotte shouted, as angry as Michael had ever seen her.

Carl was also in an ugly mood. "What did he do?!" he roared back.

"I tried to swat him, and he hit me back," Charlotte replied angrily.

Michael was very doubtful that was actually how it had gone down. He was pretty sure that his mother was just tired of his brother's disrespect.

Exactly what had happened was not important to Carl, however. He blasted in through the kitchen door, barely pausing long enough to kick off his barn boots on his rush to the cellar. He met his son halfway up the stairs.

"Where do you think you're going?" he shouted, almost out of his mind with fury!

"I was going up to tell mom I'm sorry," Carl Jr. whimpered.

"Oh, you're gonna be sorry all right!" Carl snarled. "I'll teach you to beat up on your mother!"

He grabbed his cowering son by the shoulder and threw him back down the stairs to the concrete floor.

Michael was numb with fear for his brother. This had spun way out of proportion, and something terrible was going to happen if his parents didn't get control of themselves. There were a few seconds of silence from the basement, and then, he heard a hiss and a loud snap and his brother screamed like a tortured rabbit! It went on and on until he was convinced his father would beat him unconscious or dead! How could someone even as tough as his big brother endure this for so long?

Finally, he heard his father shout, "Now git on up to your room!" Carl Jr. clawed his way up the stairs, his father right behind him, slashing him continually with his improvised "whip." When the door burst open, Carl Jr. stumbled across the kitchen floor, trying to hold up his pants with his left hand as he ran. Carl followed hard behind him, continuing to slash him viciously with the whip. Only it was not a whip. It was an electric cord! In spite of his fear of the man, Michael's hatred for the vicious animal that was his father doubled that day. He would never come near beating his cattle or even his dog the way he beat his children! Why?

*****

Auction sale day finally arrived. A carload of Charlotte's family arrived the morning of the sale, adding to the excitement and confusion of the day. One of the visitors was her brother-in-law who was the bishop of the extremely conservative church her family attended. He wore black clothes and a black felt hat and looked quite austere. Pastor Oliver arrived, sometime later, and Michael was embarrassed to see the two preachers greet each other with a handshake and a mouth-to-mouth kiss. The strict Mennonites believed in the literal practice of the Biblical instruction to "greet each other with a holy kiss." Michael thought the practice was disgusting and embarrassing. It made no sense to him that these people could rip and tear each other to shreds behind the scenes and then turn around and kiss each other in public to demonstrate their "brotherly love!"

The sale went well, and Carl was reasonably satisfied with the results except for one incident that had occurred. Someone had taken a shine to the mare that belonged to Carl Jr. and had harassed and agitated her to where she appeared to be wild and unstable in the auction ring. The man was then able to buy her much cheaper because only he knew that she was actually a tame, well-broke mare. When he was told what had happened, Carl was more upset about the horse being mistreated than about the money it had lost him.

A few days later, all the cows and machinery were gone, and the visitors had returned home. With no chores, all that was left was to pack up and head east. Carl had the neighbor with the welder make a rack for his pickup out of some old water pipes. It was crude and ugly, but it was his pride and joy for many years. He tied some old house doors to the front of the rack to block the wind and loaded the two remaining horses for the trip east. Every nook and cranny in the pickup and car were jammed full of what remained of their possessions. The church had a farewell party for them, and then the next day, they were off. Charlotte drove the car and Carl the truck with horses on the back. The older boys of course wanted to travel with the horses, so they took turns between the truck and car. Their progress was slow, but there was no deadline. They drove steadily east as the sun slowly set in the western sky behind them. Michael never looked back. He was leaving thirteen years of his life behind, and he had no desire to ever return. While there had been many good times there, the overall impression in his mind was as black as the night shadows that now wrapped around the battered old car. His mother began to sing. "Softly and tenderly Jesus is calling... Come home." He began to drift off to sleep as the hum of the wheels on the highway carried him to a new world.

EPILOGUE

The quiet man's reverie was broken by a shout as one of the basketball players sank a three-point basket, winning the game. He watched the sweaty youths exchange high fives and "good games"; then, they were gone. Gone like his own childhood and youth, he mused. He smiled as he drifted back again in time to the fateful journey from the reservation to his new life in Ohio. It had marked the end of his turbulent childhood and the beginning of his youth. He would conquer his fears and the hate and find the freedom of complete forgiveness for the man who had scarred his soul.

Although he would never have the benefit of counseling or therapy, he would learn well from the stories of others who had walked hard trails. And one dark night in the African jungle, he listened spellbound as a missionary named George told the story of how he and his fellow POWs had sentenced two of their own to death for trying to defect to the enemy. Tears rolled down the husky man's weather-beaten cheeks as he concluded with, "When we got out of that awful place, we realized what we had done. These men weren't evil. They were just weak!"

A light went on in Michael Raptor's brain. His father had not been an evil man, just a weak man! He would often wonder just how much his father had lost the night he had stood before the congregation and attributed the incredible events in their little church to Satan?

The new life would bring the Raptor boys into close contact with good men, and some of them would influence Michael's life enormously. He would meet and become close with one of his life's two heroes, Charlotte's oldest brother Donald. His other hero, Ronald Reagan, he would never meet because the man was simply too busy governing the world!

ABOUT THE AUTHOR

T.L. Hershey was born into a nomadic American family. The first 18 years of his life, the family moved 16 times. He has lived in 5 US states and one foreign country. His father tried carpentry, farming, factory work, and assorted other pursuits, but his main talent was old fashioned plastering over wood lath. His mother was a gifted artist who never pursued it as a career.

The author became acquainted with Michael Raptor in his childhood and spent much time in the Raptor home. Their close relationship would last into adulthood.

T.L. Hershey has had a lifetime love of books and writing. He discovered the joy of writing in English class as he poured himself into book reports. While the art of writing totally frustrated many of his classmates, he always declared that writing is as natural to him as breathing!

CPSIA information can be obtained
at www.ICGtesting.com
Printed in the USA
LVHW110707101119
636864LV00008B/20/P

9 781640 963948